# 2000 YEARS

## *of*

# CHARISMATIC
# CHRISTIANITY

# 2000
# YEARS
*of*
# CHARISMATIC
# CHRISTIANITY

A 21st Century Look At Church History
from a Pentecostal/Charismatic Perspective

# Eddie L. Hyatt

*Foreword by Vinson Synan*

HYATT INTERNATIONAL MINISTRIES, INC.
P. O. Box 764463
Dallas, Texas 75376
1998

Published by Hyatt International Ministries, Inc.

*Mailing Address (1998):*
P. O. BOX 764463
DALLAS, TEXAS 75376

*Official Business Address:*
P. O. BOX 78
CHICOTA, TEXAS 75425

Cover and book design by Susan Hyatt

91 92 93 94 95 96   10 9 8 7 6 5 4 3 2 1

ISBN 1-888435-09-2
Printed in the United States of America


Library of Congress
Catalog Card Number:  98-92885

## Dedication

To My Parents
Pearl Hyatt (*b.* 1918)
and
the late Rev. C. H. Hyatt (1913-1994),
whose Pentecostal testimony
inspired me
to write this book.

# CONTENTS

FOREWORD

PREFACE

ACKNOWLEDGMENTS

INTRODUCTION
1. Recovering the History of
Pentecostal/Charismatic Christianity    *1*

PART 1 - TO A.D. 100
2. The Apostolic Church    *7*

PART 2 - FROM A.D.100-325
3. The Ante-Nicene Church    *11*
4. The Decline of Spiritual Gifts
and the First Charismatic Renewal    *23*

PART 3 - FROM A.D. 325-600
5. The Impact of Constantine's Conversion on
the Charismatic Character of the Church    *35*
6. Monasticism: The Rise of
Another Charismatic Movement    *41*

PART 4 - FROM A.D. 600-1517
7. Developments in Monasticism
and the Ecclesiastical Church    *55*
8. Monastic Renewal    *61*
9. The Cathari    *69*
10. The Waldenses    *73*

PART 5 - FROM 1517-1700
11. Martin Luther and the Reformation    *77*
12. The Anabaptists    *83*
13. The French Prophets    *93*

*vii*

## Contents

14. George Fox and the Quakers  *97*
15. The Moravian Revival  *103*

PART 6 - FROM 1700-1900
16. The Methodist Revival  *107*
17. The Great Awakening  *115*
18. The Second Great Awakening  *121*
19. Edward Irving and the
    Catholic Apostolic Church  *127*
20. The 19th Century Forerunners of the Modern
    Pentecostal/Charismatic Movement  *135*

PART 7 - THE EARLY 1900S
21. Charles Parham and Bethel Bible College  *149*
22. William Seymour and the Azusa St. Revival  *155*
23. Parham and the Zion City Revival  *163*
24. The Message Spreads Around the World  *173*

PART 8 - 20TH CENTURY DEVELOPMENTS
25. Further Developments in Pentecostalism  *181*
26. The Healing Revival  *185*
27. The Latter Rain Revival  *191*
28. The Charismatic Movement  *195*
29. The Third Wave  *203*
30. A New Wave of Revival?  *207*

CONCLUSION
31. Contending for the Faith  *217*

BIBLIOGRAPHY  *220*
ABOUT THE AUTHOR  *224*

# FOREWORD

EDDIE HYATT AND SUSAN, his wife, are two of the best students I have ever taught. Their grasp of Pentecostal/Charismatic history and theology was well advanced before they enrolled in my classes at Oral Roberts University in 1990. Since that time, they have grown even more in their understanding and mastery of the subject. Eddie and Susan are one of the finest teams of husband and wife researchers that I have ever known.

His new book, *2000 Years of Charismatic Christianity*, is Hyatt's most important work to date. It is a fine historical survey of the charismatic history and nature of the church. His treatment of the origins and fate of the cessation of the charismata theory is well researched and convincingly presented. As the subtitle suggests, this volume is indeed "a 21st century look at Church History from a Pentecostal/Charismatic perspective." Of particular value and interest are Hyatt's sections on Charles Fox Parham, the formulator of Pentecostal theology, and the crucial part played by followers of Alexander Dowie who left Zion City to found important Pentecostal movements around the world.

Hyatt's work is another in a stream of scholarly works that are driving nails in the coffin of the Warfield theory of the cessation of the miraculous signs, wonders, and miracles after the end of the apostolic age. He writes well and convincingly. I feel that this book brings together the most recent research on the subject and presents it in a popular way that any reader can understand.

I commend 2000 Years of Charismatic Christianity to all who look for deeper understanding of the modern Pentecostal/Charismatic movements that have exploded in the 20th Century to become the second largest family of Christians in the world.

Dean of the School of Divinity            VINSON SYNAN
Regent University, Virginia Beach, Virginia

# PREFACE

THE INSPIRATION FOR THIS BOOK came from my roots in classical Pentecostalism and my love for history. Additional motivation arose when I became aware of the lack of available information about charismatic believers and movements in church history. My first church history course in a Pentecostal Bible school, to my surprise, seemed to survey the history of the Roman Catholic and Reformation churches. Pentecostal/Charismatic people and themes were not dealt with until the twentieth century. Was the Holy Spirit, in fact, absent from 1800 years of Church history?

As I began a serious search, I discovered that the charismatic dimension of the Spirit's activity was not missing from the Church's past. Instead, a prevailing bias against charismatic gifts often influenced modern historians either to ignore the gifts of the Holy Spirit or to speak of them disparagingly. Further, I discovered that Pentecostals and Charismatics, because of a lack of scholarly research, often accepted the determinations of non-charismatic historians.

As my search continued, I discovered the perennial conflict between the spontaneity of the Spirit and the rigid structures of the institution. This often resulted in the institutional Church labeling as heretics those who championed the freedom of the Spirit and suppressing or destroying their writings. This, of course, contributed to the lack of data about the Holy Spirit's activity in history.

In this book, I fill in some of the gaps by chronicling Pentecostal/Charismatic people and movements. This study is neither exhaustive nor critical. Its purpose is to show that Pentecostal/Charismatics do have a legitimate history. It also suggests that instead of being on the fringes of orthodox Christianity, Pentecostal/Charismatic Christianity is in the mainstream of both biblical and historic Christianity.

# ACKNOWLEDGMENTS

ANYONE WHO HAS EVER WRITTEN a book understands what a cooperative effort it is, and this book is no exception. In the first place, if the people and movements about which I have written had not courageously followed the Lord, there would have been no substance or reason to write. On a more personal level, if many people had not partnered with me in one way or another, this book would have remained in the realm of dreams.

I want to thank the many friends and partners of Hyatt International Ministries for their prayers and financial support, both while I was writing and when it came time to meet printing costs of the first edition. I am particularly grateful to Margaret Bridge of New Brunswick, Canada; Pastor Bob Nichols and Calvary Cathedral International of Fort Worth, Texas; and Evangelists Dale and Jean Gentry also of Fort Worth. These people provided significant gifts which helped make this book a reality.

I want to thank Dr. Benjamin Crandall, President of Zion Bible Institute in Barrington, Rhode Island, who arranged my teaching schedule during the 1991-92 school year so that I was able to spend four days each week in research and writing.

I also want to thank Esther Rollins, who at the tender age of 84, did the proof-reading of the first edition which is the basis of this new edition.

I am grateful to my wife, Susan, who is a constant encouragement to me. She contributed her editorial skills to the book and provided expert historical/theological reflections. Her diligence in preparing the camera-ready copies of both editions gave the final thrust that made this dream a reality.

## CHAPTER 1

# Recovering the History of Charismatic Christianity

CHARISMATIC CHRISTIANITY is not solely a twentieth century phenomenon. It has been around since Jesus walked the earth 2000 years ago. In the twentieth century, however, there has been a veritable explosion of charismatic Christianity. Beginning with the Pentecostal Movement in 1901, and revitalized by the Charismatic Movement beginning in 1960 and the Third Wave beginning around 1980, this explosion of charismatic Christianity has gained momentum and permeated every facet of church life. Not since the first century, has there been such a wide-spread emphasis on the Holy Spirit and His gifts.

Is this expression of spirituality simply heresy and fanaticism, as some would charge? Is it merely a marginal expression of true Christianity, as others would suggest? Or is it, in fact, a restoration of true biblical Christianity?

Legitimate questions have also been raised regarding the historicity of this dynamic form of Christianity. Has it reappeared suddenly in this century with no historical link to the first century Church, as some contend? Or does it, in fact, have historical precedent?

And why is it called *charismatic*? The word *charismatic* is derived from the Greek word *charisma*, the New Testament word for *spiritual gift*. *Charisma*, or its plural form, *charismata*,

1

is the word Paul uses in 1 Corinthians 12:1-11 when he discusses the gifts of the Holy Spirit, such as speaking in tongues, gifts of healings, miracles, and prophecy. For this reason, any group, church, or movement that espouses this dynamic dimension of the Holy Spirit and His gifts may be called *charismatic*. Even though they may be known historically as Quakers, Methodists, or Pentecostals, their penchant for the dynamism of the Holy Spirit and His gifts qualifies them to be designated *charismatic*. For the same reason, the first century Church may also be called a *charismatic* church.

## What's the Difference?

The question has often been asked: What is the difference between modern *Pentecostals* and *Charismatics*? Perhaps the chief distinction is related to the different historical origins of the two movements. The Pentecostal Movement began in 1901 in Bethel Bible School in Topeka, Kansas, where an outpouring of the Holy Spirit occurred and the classical Pentecostal doctrine of speaking in tongues as the biblical evidence of Spirit baptism was formulated and activated. The beginning of the modern Charismatic Movement, on the other hand, is usually identified with the 1960 announcement by Dennis Bennett, rector of St. Mark's Episcopal Church in Van Nuys, California, that he had been baptized in the Holy Spirit and had spoken in tongues.

Another important distinction is the fact that the Pentecostal Movement was rejected by the existing churches with the result that since that time, over 11,000 new Pentecostal denominations have been formed world-wide.[1] In contrast, the Charismatic Movement achieved a remarkable degree of acceptance in the traditional churches where it was often referred to as a *renewal*. Nonetheless, over 3000 Charismatic denominations have already been formed since the 1960s.[2]

In spite of these differences, statistician David Barrett notes that an "underlying unity" pervades the entire twentieth century movement. For this reason, he has coined the phrase *Pentecostal/Charismatic* to refer to the work of the Holy Spirit throughout the earth in this century. He views the Pentecostal, Charismatic, and Third Wave Movements as "one single cohesive movement into which a vast proliferation of all kinds of individuals and communities have been drawn."[3]

## Phenomenal Growth

Amazingly, just one hundred years ago, not one Pentecostal/Charismatic congregation, as we understand the term today, existed. Now, less than a century later, Pentecostal and Charismatic churches and denominations dot the religious landscape and constitute the most dynamic and fastest growing segment of Christendom.

This astounding growth was highlighted by a 1980 Gallup Poll published in *Christianity Today*. The poll indicated that 19 percent of the total population of the United States, or about 50 million people, identified themselves as Pentecostal or Charismatic Christians. The same poll reported that 22 percent of all Protestants claimed to be Pentecostal or Charismatic, while 18 percent of Roman Catholics identified themselves with the movement. This phenomenal growth is one of the main reasons that well-known Harvard theologian, Harvey Cox, is willing to say that Pentecostalism is "reshaping religion in the twenty-first century."[4]

## The Challenge of Historical Legitimacy

One criticism often directed at modern Pentecostals and

Charismatics is that they have no tradition or history. The argument goes something like this: The Church has been in existence for 2000 years but Pentecostals and Charismatics have been around for less than one hundred years. This purported lack of history would seem to indicate that the movement is, at best, peripheral to orthodox Christianity.

This challenge of historical legitimacy is usually answered in one of two ways by proponents of the movement. Classical Pentecostals have taken a *restorationist* approach, commonly looking upon themselves as representing a restoration of the purity and power of the first century, apostolic Church. From this perspective, the 1800 intervening years are regarded as years of corruption and spiritual demise.[5] More recently, some Pentecostals and Charismatics have been unwilling to skip 1800 years of church history and have taken a *traditionalist* approach. They seek to fill the perceived historical vacuum by forming traditional, ecclesiastical offices in the structure of their churches and by instituting traditional liturgies into their worship services.[6] Such measures are motivated, in part, by attempts to establish a continuity with the past through identifying with the traditional, institutional churches.

Neither the *restorationist* approach nor the *traditionalist* approach, however, adequately answers the historical question. The fact is that Pentecostals and Charismatics do have a legitimate history. It is a history found in the various revival and renewal movements that have emerged constantly in the life of the Church. Because these were often condemned or marginalized by the institutional church, their history has been submerged or misconstrued. It is, therefore, a history in need of discovery and full recovery.

## The Road to Historical Recovery

This volume brings together, under one cover, a number of elements recovered through scholarly, historical research. It chronicles some of the courageous people and movements from the Day of Pentecost to the closing days of the twentieth century. In so doing, it traces historical predecessors of the modern charismatic explosion. It connects the modern revival with the first century Church.

This study is by no means exhaustive; nevertheless, its benefits are many. Permitted to do so, it can inform the earnest seeker of the dynamic activity of the Holy Spirit thoughout the history of the Church. In addition, it can instruct those who would learn from the past. It can also inspire further research and promote further awareness and understanding of the rich history that rightfully belongs to every Pentecostal/Charismatic believer.

Finally, the data in this book confirms that modern Pentecostals/Charismatics do have an exciting and legitimate history. Their link with the past is not an organizational link; it is, instead, one of like biblical faith that continues to demonstrate the spiritual power of the first century, apostolic Church. Indeed, that the Pentecostal/Charismatic revival of this century is orthodox Christianity is confirmed not only by the New Testament itself, but also by the existence of 2000 years of charismatic Christianity.

---

### Notes

[1] Burgess, Stanley M. and Gary B. McGee, *Dictionary of Pentecostal and Charismatic Movements* (Grand Rapids: Zondervan, 1988), 811.

[2] *Dictionary of Pentecostal and Charismatic Movements*, 811.

[3] *Dictionary of Pentecostal and Charismatic Movements*, 810.

[4] These words occur in the subtitle of Harvey Cox, *Fire From Heaven: The Rise of Pentecostal Spirituality and the Reshaping of Religion in the Twenty-first Century* (Reading, MA; New York: Addison-Wesley, 1995).

[5] See "Roundtable," *Pentecostal Evangel,* no. 4220 (Aug. 13, 1995): 8, where George O. Wood, an executive presbyter of the Assemblies of God, affirms the early Pentecostal restorationist approach to history. He says, "We were willing to skip, if we could 19 centuries of Christian history and say, 'While we thank God for what was accomplished by Him in history, our goal is not to be in the pattern of church tradition. We simply want to go back to the book of Acts and rediscover what the Early Church had and possess it so we can be the instrument God uses in our generation.'"

[6] See Paul Thigpen, "Ancient Altars, Pentecostal Fire," *Ministries Today,* Nov./Dec. 1992: 43-51.

CHAPTER 2

# The Apostolic Church

THE CHURCH OF THE FIRST CENTURY was a charismatic church. Luke, who recorded its history in the book of Acts, faithfully included the abundance of supernatural phenomena that characterized its life and ministry. Speaking in tongues and prophecy, healings and miracles, and all the other *charismata* were common—even anticipated as the norm—(Acts 1:8; 10:19; 13:2). It was this dynamic activity of the Holy Spirit in the personal, individual lives of the believers and in the corporate life of the Church, rather than organizational structure, that provided the basis for its life, community, and mission.

As believers carried the Gospel from Jerusalem into the Greco-Roman world, this charismatic character continued to be the norm for the new churches which sprang up through their ministries. This is obvious from Acts as well as from Paul's epistles where he speaks freely of miracles and spiritual gifts. He declares that he "fully preached" the Gospel of Christ to the Gentiles "in mighty signs and wonders, by the power of the Spirit of God" (Rom. 15:19). The Corinthian letters, in particular, indicate that the assembled churches relied on the spontaneity of the Spirit rather than on official authority for the life and direction of their meetings.

These facts led Hans von Campenhausen to describe the early Church's vision of Christian community as "one of free fellowship, developing through the living interplay of spiritual gifts and ministries, without the benefit of official authority or

7

responsible elders."[1] Roman Catholic theologian, Hans Kung, concurs, suggesting that the church at Corinth "knew of neither *episkopoi* (bishops) nor *presbuteros* (elders) nor any kind of ordination but only the free and spontaneous charisms."[2] He then points out that, according to Paul, they were provided with all that was necessary.[3] Rudolph Bultmann agrees and insists that in the New Testament Church "The chief persons of authority are those endowed with spiritual gifts."[4]

James D. G. Dunn, in his book *Jesus and the Spirit*, demonstrates that the earliest Christian churches looked to the immediate presence of the Holy Spirit for their community and life, rather than to organizational structure and formality. He also points out that, apart from Phil. 1:1, "Paul never addresses himself to a leadership group within a community."[5] For Dunn the implication is plain: "If leadership was required, Paul assumed that the charismatic Spirit would provide it."[6]

### Offices or Functions?

The Pastoral Epistles, which are from a later period of Paul's life, seem to reveal a more formal structure of church life. The term *presbuteros* (elder) is used for the first time by Paul, and qualifications are given for those who would serve as *episkopoi* (bishops) or *diakonoi* (deacons). Adolph Harnack suggests, however, that *presbuteros* or *elder* may simply denote *the old* as opposed to *the young*, and John Knox insists, "We are not dealing with formal offices, but with functions for which persons were as certainly spiritually endowed as for prophecy and healing."[7] Kung agrees and says that the appointing of elders "must not be seen as the beginning of a clerical ruling system." He points out that the emergence of elders/bishops must be understood in the context "of the fundamentally charismatic structure of the Church."[8]

## Greater or Lesser Works?

The early Church's emphasis on the *charismata* should not be surprising since Jesus taught His disciples to expect the power and dynamism of the Spirit in their lives and ministries. On one occasion, He advised them that when the Spirit came, they would be enabled to do the same works that He was doing and even greater works (Jn. 14:12). The early Church's expectation of supernatural ministry was, therefore, rooted in the life and teachings of Jesus Himself. Dunn says, "As He was charismatic, so were many, if not all of the earliest believers."[9]

But what happened after the first century—after the decease of the original apostles? Did the Pentecostal/Charismatic gifts suddenly cease? Were the revelatory gifts displaced by the formation of the New Testament canon of Scripture? Did the supernatural character of the Church vanish altogether after the close of the so-called apostolic age of the first century?

In retrospect, it can be seen that there was a gradual demise of the charismatic character of the Church and a corresponding rise of organizational structure. Nevertheless, spiritual gifts continued to be a vital part of the life of the Church after the first century. Post-apostolic writings reveal no knowledge or expectation of their cessation at some point in time. Those who succeeded the apostles as leaders in the Church have, instead, left clear testimony of the continued work of the Spirit's gifts and power during their time.

## Notes

[1] Hans von Campenhausen, *Ecclesiastical Authority and Spiritual Power in the Churches of the First Three Centuries* (Stanford: Stanford Univ., 1969), 58.

[2] Hans Kung, "What is the Essence of Apostolic Succession?," *Apostolic Succession:Rethinking A Barrier To Unity*, ed. Hans Kung (New York: Paulist Press, 1968), 35.

[3] Kung, "What is the Essence of Apostolic Succession," 34.

[4] Rudolph Bultmann, *New Testament Theology*, 2 vols. (New York: Charles Scribner, 1965), 2: 97.

[5] James D.G. Dunn, *Jesus and the Spirit* (Philadelphia: Westminster, 1975), 291.

[6] Dunn, *Jesus and the Spirit*, 285.

[7] John Knox, "The Ministry in the Primitive Church," *The Ministry in Historical Perspective*, ed. Richard H. Niebuhr and Daniel D. Williams (New York: Harper and Row, 1956), 10.

[8] Hans Kung, *The Church* (Garden City, NY: Image Books, 1976), 249.

[9] Dunn, *Jesus and the Spirit*, 92.

## CHAPTER 3

# The Ante-Nicene Church

### Justin Martyr

JUSTIN MARTYR (A.D. 100-165) is regarded as the foremost apologist of the second century. Born of pagan parents near the biblical town of Shechem, he became a brilliant, wandering philosopher. He was never able to satisfy his heart's hunger for truth, however, until one day, while walking on a beach, he met an elderly man who directed him to the Scriptures. These, the man declared, constituted the true philosophy. Justin was convinced and converted. He went on to open a Christian school in Rome.

Justin was obviously familiar with the miraculous gifts of the Holy Spirit. In his *Dialogue with Trypho*, he writes, "For the prophetical gifts remain with us even to the present time."[1] Later, in the same work, he says, "Now it is possible to see among us women and men who possess gifts of the Spirit of God."[2] In another work called *The Second Apology of Justin*, he speaks of the ability of Christians in his day to cast out demons and minister healing. He writes,

> For numberless demoniacs throughout the whole world, and in your city, many of our Christian men exorcising them in the name of Jesus Christ, who was crucified under Pontius Pilate, have healed and do heal, rendering helpless and driving the possessing devils out of the men.[3]

Justin Martyr, therefore, clearly testifies that Christians in the second century were continuing to exercise authority over demons and sickness. He also indicates that both men and women were exercising other gifts of the Spirit as well. Furthermore, never does he suggest that he expects these gifts to cease at some point in time.

### Irenaeus

Irenaeus (A.D. 125-200), bishop of Lyons, is best known for his writings against gnosticism and other major heresies of his day. Born in the city of Smyrna, he was a student of Polycarp, a disciple of the apostle John. From his writings, it is obvious that the miraculous gifts of the Holy Spirit were still prominent in the life of the Church of his day.

In his work *Against Heresies*, Irenaeus shows the fallacy of certain gnostics who claimed that Jesus was a phantasm with no real physical body and that He performed his works "simply in appearance." Irenaeus refutes this claim by pointing to the works that followers of Jesus were performing even then. He says,

> For some do certainly and truly drive out devils, so that those who have been thus cleansed from evil spirits frequently both believe [in Christ], and join themselves to the Church. Others have foreknowledge of things to come: they see visions and utter prophetic expressions. Others still heal the sick by laying their hands upon them, and they are made whole.

Irenaeus also speaks of the dead being raised.

> Yea, moreover, as I have said, the dead even have been raised up, and remained among us for many years. And what shall I more say? It is not possible to name the number of gifts which the Church [scattered] throughout the whole world, has received from God in the name of Jesus Christ.[4]

12

Also testifying that believers were still speaking in tongues in his day, Irenaeus writes,

> In like manner we do also hear many brethren in the Church who possess prophetic gifts and who through the Spirit speak all kinds of languages, and bring to light for the general benefit the hidden things of men, and declare the mysteries of God.[5]

The life and writings of Irenaeus reach almost to the third century. His writings are a powerful testimony to the widespread knowledge and practice of spiritual gifts in the Church of his time. As with Justin Martyr, Irenaeus in no way indicated that he expected the *charismata* to cease.

## Tertullian

Tertullian (A.D. 160-240), a native of Carthage, was converted in A.D. 192. At the time, he was already proficient in law and the philosophic systems of his day. Skilled in both Greek and Latin, he wrote extensively in the latter. With this background, he quickly became a presbyter in Carthage, an influential leader in the Church, and the foremost apologist of the Western church. In his incisive, potent writings against hostile rulers and heretical sects of his day, he formulated theological concepts that gained him the title *Father of Latin Theology*. His writings also reveal a personal acquaintance with the supernatural gifts of the Holy Spirit including speaking in tongues.

In *A Treatise on the Soul*, Tertullian says, "For seeing that we acknowledge the spiritual *charismata*, or gifts, we too have merited the attainment of the prophetic gift."[6] He goes on to tell of a woman in his congregation "whose lot it has been to be favored with sundry gifts of revelation." According to Tertullian, she often experienced visitations from angels and from the Lord Himself. In addition, she often knew the secrets of people's hearts and was able to give answers to some of their deepest needs, including physical healing. Tertullian says, "All her communications are examined with the most scrupulous care in order that their truth may be probed."[7]

In *To Scapula*, Tertullian relates specific instances of healing and deliverance from demonic oppression. He concludes, "And heaven knows how many distinguished men, to say nothing of the common people, have been cured either of devils or of their sicknesses."[8]

In *Against Marcion*, written to counter the heretic Marcion, Tertullian reveals both his acquaintance with speaking in tongues and his belief that the supernatural gifts of the Spirit were a sign of orthodoxy. This is obvious in his challenge to Marcion.

> Let Marcion then exhibit, as gifts of his god, some prophets such as have not spoken by human sense, but with the Spirit of God, such as have predicted things to come, and have made manifest the secrets of the heart; let him produce a psalm, a vision, a prayer—only let it be by the spirit, in an ecstasy, that is, in a rapture, whenever an interpretation of tongues has occurred to him. Now all these signs are forthcoming from my side without any difficulty.[9]

In *On Baptism*, Tertullian supports a work of the Spirit in the believer subsequent to conversion. He writes, "Not that in the water we obtain the Spirit; but in the water we are cleansed and prepared for the Holy Spirit." He also states that following baptism "the hand is laid on us, invoking and inviting the Holy Spirit through benediction."[10] Undoubtedly this refers to the apostolic custom of laying hands on new converts for the reception of the Holy Spirit.[11]

Tertullian's testimony, therefore, demonstrates that in the third century, spiritual gifts were still prominent in the Church. His view of a subsequent work of the Holy Spirit after baptism is especially interesting in light of the modern Pentecostal/Charismatic Movement which also teaches an empowerment subsequent to conversion. Like others of his era, Tertullian gives no indication that he expects these gifts to cease.

## Origen

Origen (A.D. 185-284), a prolific and influential writer, was the Church's first systematic theologian. When Origen was sixteen years old, his father, a devout believer, was martyred. In Alexandria, Egypt, when he was eighteen, Origen was appointed leader of a prominent Christian school founded to instruct converts from paganism.

In *Against Celsus*, Origen speaks of the miracles being performed in his day through the power of Jesus' name. His testimony indicates that he is personally involved in many of these miracles.

> Some give evidence of their having received through this faith a marvelous power by the cures which they perform, invoking no other name over those who need their help than that of the God of all things, and of Jesus, along with a mention of his history. For by these means we too have seen many persons freed from grievous calamities, and from distractions of mind, and madness, and countless other ills, which could not be cured neither by men nor devils.[12]

Further in this work, Origen quotes a charge which Celsus, a pagan writer, had leveled against Christians. Celsus criticizes the Christians' claim of inspiration through the prophetic gift and then cynically quotes portions of prophetic utterances which he had heard. He then says, "To these promises are added strange, fanatical, and quite unintelligible words, of which no rational person can find the meaning."[13] If this statement refers to speaking in tongues, as some believe, then it is a testimony from one outside the Church that speaking in tongues commonly occurred in the Church at that time. The context of the argument also clearly indicates that prophetic utterances were still common enough among Christians that a pagan writer was aware of the practice.

Origen obviously recognized the reality and value of praying in tongues, and gives further evidence of this in his commentary on Romans 8:26 where he links praying in the Spirit with praying in tongues. Cecil M. Robeck, notes, "Origen must have held that prayer in tongues existed in his day, and it was thought to be beneficial in that it was through this type of prayer that the Spirit interceded exceedingly before God."[14]

Origen, like Tertullian, shows his belief in a work of the Holy Spirit subsequent to regeneration. In *De Principiis*, he speaks of God breathing into Adam the breath [Spirit] of life, adding that this cannot refer to all men, but only to those who have been made new in Christ. Then he says,

> For this reason was the grace and revelation of the Holy Spirit bestowed by the imposition of the apostles' hands after baptism. Our Savior also, after the resurrection, when old things had already passed away, and all things had become new . . . His apostles also being renewed by faith in His resurrection, says "Receive the Holy Spirit."[15]

Origen was the first early church father to indicate that supernatural ministry was becoming less common. He points to the abundance of supernatural signs in the ministries of Christ and the apostolic Church. Then he remarks, "But since that time these signs have diminished." He cites the lack of holiness and purity among the Christians of his day as the reason.[16]

Origen, therefore, was familiar with the miraculous ministry of the Holy Spirit, including speaking in tongues. He also clearly teaches a work of the Spirit subsequent to conversion. In addition, while he indicates a diminishing of charismatic activity, he attributes this, not to a divine decree, but to a lack of holiness among the Christians of his day.

### Novatian

Novatian (A.D. 210-280) was a presbyter of the church in Rome and a respected theologian. He was apparently noted for his compassion and holiness, for in a polemic written against him, his opponent says that Novatian "wept over the sins of his neighbors as if they were his own, bore the burdens of the brethren, as the Apostle exhorts, and strengthened those who were weak in divine faith."[17] Novatian became embroiled in a controversy with Cornelius, bishop of Rome, because of the leniency Cornelius was showing toward Christians who had "lapsed" during persecution. The matter was never fully resolved and eventually Novatian became a rival bishop of Rome.

The movement Novatian spawned gained momentum and spread quickly especially in the eastern Mediterranean and North Africa. Adherents called themselves *Cathari*, meaning *pure ones*, to distinguish themselves from other professing Christians whom they considered carnal and impure. Other groups in church history with similar emphasis also adopted this designation. In the eighteenth and nineteenth centuries, the Holiness Movement maintained similar priorities.

Perhaps the most important of Novatian's surviving works is his treatise, *The Trinity*. In it he discusses his familiarity with the supernatural ministry of the Holy Spirit.

> This is he [the Holy Spirit] who places prophets in the Church, instructs teachers, directs tongues, gives powers and healings, does wonderful works, offers discrimination of spirits, affords powers of government, suggests counsels, and orders and arranges whatever other gifts there are of charismata; and thus making the Lord's Church everywhere, and in all, perfected and completed.[18]

For Novatian, then, the Holy Spirit was the source of life and order for the Church. He clearly accepts as normal Christian experiences such phenomena as healings, miracles, and tongues. His belief in the *charismata* was not an issue since the Church of his day still recognized the gifts as a vital part of normal Christianity.

Novatian's emphasis on moral purity, coupled with the testimony of Origen, indicates that moral decline among Christians was a trend in both eastern and western sectors of the Church. This moral decline produced contention and strife in the Church, and eventually the official institution sided against those who advocated strict moral purity. Succeeding generations would interpret this stance on morality as a primary cause of the Church's loss of spiritual power.

## Cyprian

Cyprian (A.D. 195-258), a prosperous Carthaginian by birth, enjoyed the benefits of a good education in rhetoric and law. When he became a Christian in about 246, he quickly gained prominence. Within two years, he had become bishop of Carthage, a position he held until his martyrdom in 258.

That Cyprian was aware of the *charismata* seems evident in that he was an avid reader of Tertullian. Cyprian's secretary told Jerome that Cyprian never passed a day without reading from Tertullian and was accustomed to asking for him with the words, "Hand me the Master."[19]

Cyprian, by his own testimony, often experienced supernatural visions. His explanation for actions taken by his congregation during a time of persecution was, "It seemed best to us through many and clear visions."[20] These visions, in fact, occurred throughout the Christian community.

> For beside the visions of the night, even in the daytime, the innocent age of boys [innocent children] is among us filled with the Holy Spirit, seeing in an ecstasy with their eyes, and hearing and speaking those things whereby the Lord condescends to warn and instruct us.[21]

While bishop of Carthage, Cyprian became embroiled in a controversy with Stephen, bishop of Rome. Stephen maintained that those previously baptized by heretics would not need to be rebaptized when they returned to the Church. Cyprian strongly disagreed and staunchly insisted they must again submit to baptism. In the course of the debate, Cyprian's position that the Holy Spirit is received subsequent to the work of regeneration becomes clear. He sees regeneration as taking place in true baptism and the reception of the Holy Spirit as occurring thereafter through the laying on of hands.[22] He says, "For he who has been sanctified, his sins being put away in baptism, and has been spiritually reformed into a new man, has become fitted for receiving the Holy Spirit."[23]

Cyprian compares the two events, regeneration and reception of the Spirit, with events in God's creation of Adam. Adam was first formed and then God breathed into him the breath [Spirit] of life. In parallel fashion, Cyprian concludes that a person is first born [again] and then filled with the Holy Spirit.

19

One is not born by the imposition of hands when he receives the Holy Ghost, but in baptism, that so, being already born, he may receive the Holy Spirit, even as it happened to the first man Adam. For first God formed him and then breathed into his nostrils the breath of life.[24]

Cyprian's writings provide further evidence that the supernatural ministry of the Holy Spirit was still considered a normal part of the life and ministry of the third-century Church. His belief in a filling of the Holy Spirit subsequent to conversion also attests to the widespread acceptance of this view in the third century. Like other writers of his era, Cyprian expresses no awareness of a theory of cessation.

## Other Early Testimonies

Other early Christian writings confirm the continued presence of spiritual gifts in the churches. For example, the *Didache*, probably written at the beginning of the second century, recognizes the legitimacy of the prophetic ministry and gives instruction concerning how to distinguish between true and false prophets. *The Shepherd of Hermes*, written during the early second century, is based on the supernatural revelations and visions of the author. Ignatius, bishop of Antioch, in his letter *To The Philadelphians* written at the beginning of the second century, reminds his readers of the prophetic message he had spoken in their midst during a recent visit.[25]

## Conclusion

These testimonies clearly demonstrate that spiritual gifts, including speaking in tongues, continued to be common in the Church from the Day of Pentecost up to the beginning of the fourth century. Episcopal scholar, Morton Kelsey, is correct in saying, "These men were well aware of Paul's list of the gifts of the Spirit and what it included. In no place do they suggest that any of them had dropped away."[26] Origen indicates their decline, but not their cessation.

The patristic testimonies also indicate that the reception of the Holy Spirit was considered an event subsequent to conversion initiated by laying on of hands. This was obviously a continuation of the apostolic custom recorded in the book of Acts. This testimony indicates that, for at least the first three centuries, the Church followed this apostolic custom of conversion followed by the reception of the Holy Spirit.[27]

---

### Notes

[1] Justin Martyr, *Dialogue With Trypho* vol. 1 of *The Ante-Nicene Christian Library*, ed. Rev. Alexander Roberts and James Donaldson (Edinburgh: T & T Clark, 1874), 240.

[2] Justin Martyr, *Dialogue With Trypho*, 243.

[3] Justin Martyr, *The Second Apology of Justin* vol. 1 of *The Ante-Nicene Christian Library*, ed. Rev. Alexander Roberts and James Donaldson (Edinburgh: T & T Clark, 1874), 190.

[4] Irenaeus, *Against Heresies*, vol. 1 of *The Ante-Nicene Christian Library*, ed. Rev. Alexander Roberts and James Donaldson (Edinburgh: T & T Clark, 1874), 409.

[5] Irenaeus, *Against Heresies*, 531.

[6] Tertullian, *A Treatise on the Soul*, vol. 3 of *The Ante-Nicene Christian Library*, ed. Rev. Alexander Roberts and James Donaldson (Edinburgh: T & T Clark, 1874), 189.

[7] Tertullian, *A Treatise on the Soul*, 188.

[8] Tertullian, *Apologetic Works*, vol. 10 of *The Fathers of the Church*, trans. William P. Le Saint (London: Longmans & Green, 1950), 121.

[9] Tertullian, *Against Marcion*, vol. 3 of *The Ante-Nicene Christian Library*, ed. Rev. Alexander Roberts and James Donaldson (Edinburgh: T & T Clark, 1874), 447.

[10] Tertullian, *On Baptism*, vol. 3 of *The Ante-Nicene Christian Library*, ed. Rev. Alexander Roberts and James Donaldson (Edinburgh: T & T Clark, 1874), 672.

[11] See Acts 8:14-17, 9:17, and 19:5-6.

[12] Origen, *Against Celsus*, vol. 4 of *The Ante-Nicene Christian Library*, ed. Rev. Alexander Roberts and James Donaldson (Edinburgh: T & T Clark, 1874), 473.

[13] Origen, *Against Celsus*, 614.

[14] Cecil M. Robeck, "Origen's Treatment of the *Charismata*," *Charismatic Experiences in History* (Peabody, MA: Hendrickson, 1985), 120.

[15] Origen, *Origen De Principiis*, vol. 4 of *The Ante-Nicene Christian Library*, ed. Rev. Alexander Roberts and James Donaldson (Edinburgh: T & T Clark, 1874), 254.

[16] Origen, *Against Celsus*, 614.

[17] Russell J. DeSimone trans., "Novatian: The Trinity," *The Fathers of the Church* (Washington D.C.: Consortium, 1974), 4.

[18] DeSimone trans., "Novatian: The Trinity," 4.

[19] Jerome, *Illustrious Men of the Church*, vol. 3 of *Nicene and Post Nicene Fathers of the Christian Church*, 2nd Series, eds. Philip Schaff and Henry Wace (Grand Rapids: Eerdmans, 1978), 373.

[20] Cyprian, *Letters*, vol. 51 of *The Fathers of the Church*, ed. Roy Joseph Defarrai (Washington D.C.: Catholic Univ. American Press, 1964), 161.

[21] Cyprian, *The Epistles of Cyprian* vol. 5 of *The Ante-Nicene Christian Library*, ed. Rev. Alexander Roberts and James Donaldson (Edinburgh: T & T Clark, 1874), 290.

[22] Cyprian does not seem to advocate a mechanical baptismal regeneration. He says, "For water alone is not able to cleanse away sins and to sanctify a man unless he have also the Holy Spirit." Cyprian sees authentic baptism taking place in the context of faith and proper church authority.

[23] Cyprian, *The Epistles of Cyprian*, 387.

[24] Cyprian, *The Epistles of Cyprian*, 388.

[25] Michael W. Holmes, ed., *The Apostolic Fathers*, trans. J. B. Lightfoot and J. R. Harmer (Grand Rapids: Baker, 1989), 108.

[26] Morton T. Kelsey, *Tongue Speaking* (Garden City: Doubleday, 1964), 55.

[27] See Eusebius, *The History of the Church*, trans. G. A. Williamson (New York: Dorset Press, 1965), 282-283, who, writing at the beginning of the fourth century, notes that a certain bishop, even though he had been baptized, could not have received the Holy Spirit because he had not received confirmation, or the laying on of hands.

# CHAPTER 4

# Decline of Spiritual Gifts and the First Charismatic Renewal

## Institutionalism and Bishops

SPIRITUAL GIFTS CONTINUED to be manifest after the first century. As institutionalism increasingly dominated the life and ministry of the Church, however, their prevalence and influence gradually diminished. *Institutionalism* is an emphasis on organization at the expense of other factors. In the Church, such an emphasis or over-emphasis on organization, always comes at the expense of the life and freedom of the Spirit. Professor James L. Ash, Jr. says that virtually all historians of Christianity agree that the institutionalization of the early Church was accompanied by the demise of the charismatic gifts.[1]

The move toward institutionalism in the early Church arose as a means of defense against persecution from the state and imposition of error from heretical sects such as Gnosticism and Marcionism. Reacting to these threats, the Church formalized worship and centralized power in the bishop. Unfortunately, this move toward organizational structure brought about a change in the very meaning of the word *bishop*.

The word *bishop* is derived from the Greek word *episcopas* which, in its verb form means *to watch over* and, therefore, *to superintend* or *to oversee*. Not unique to the New Testament, it was used in the larger Greco-Roman world of the first century in reference to individuals who functioned as tutors, inspectors, scouts, watchmen, and superintendents.[2] In the apostolic Church, the word was used to describe the function of oversight given to certain individuals in matters related to the churches. Acts 20:17, 28 and Titus 1:5-7 show that the same individuals who are known as *episcopas* are also referred to as *elders* who are expected to shepherd or *pastor* the flock.

With the growing emphasis on organizational structure, *episcopas* evolved into a separate and distinct office with increasing prestige and power. This change is borne out in the writings of Ignatius, bishop of Caesarea, who in all his writings (ca. A.D. 110), seems preoccupied with defending and promoting the authority and prestige of the bishop. In *To the Smyrneans*, for example, Ignatius declares, "only that Eucharist which is under the bishop is to be considered valid." He asserted that apart from the bishop, it is not lawful "either to baptize or to hold a love-feast."[3] In his letter *To the Trallians*, he admonishes his readers to "do nothing without the bishop."[4]

Ash describes Ignatius' attempt to garner such authority for himself and for the office of the bishop as "a novelty."[5] Indeed, when compared with the writings of the New Testament, it is obvious that Ignatius has taken a new path in church government. In his classic work, *The Primitive Church*, Burnett Streeter says.

> What nobody questions, nobody defends; over-enthusiastic defense implies the existence of strong oppostion. The principle which Ignatius is so concerned to uphold is one by no means universally recognized.[6]

History demonstrates that the institutional trend advocated by Ignatius continued, culminating in the ecclesiasticism of the medieval Roman Catholic Church and in its monarchical bishop. This meant that outward ecclesiastical forms of both office and ritual came to be valued over personal, spiritual experiences. It also meant that spontaneous manifestations of the Holy Spirit became less and less desirable, especially by those in authority. It is for this reason that Ash, in answer to the popular notion that the charismatic gifts were replaced by the New Testament Canon, declares, "The bishops, not the Canon, expelled prophecy."[7]

For those who embraced this emphasis on organizational structure, spiritual authority was no longer seen as residing in the person with the spiritual gift. That authority now resided, instead, in the one occupying the ecclesiastical office. This generated mounting tensions between those who continued to embrace spiritual gifts and those who preferred the emerging organizational structure.

Those who desired the freedom and spontaneity of the Spirit felt squelched by the growing ritual and formality. On the other hand, church leaders, who by now might occupy the office without the spiritual gift, felt uncomfortable with the charismatics' claim of direct communion with God. The issue came to a head in the latter half of the second century when Montanus began to reassert the importance of spiritual gifts in the Church, particularly the gift of prophecy.

## Montanus

Montanus was born in Phrygia during the first half of the second century and at one time may have been a bishop. Although a convert from paganism, as a Christian, he was orthodox in his faith accepting all the books of the Canon as well as the *Rule of Faith*.[8] He was "distinguished in working signs and miracles," and even his enemies admitted that "both his life and doctrine were holy and blameless."[9]

Montanus was concerned about the growing formalism in the Church and the increasing moral laxity among its members. Around A.D. 172, therefore, he began to assert the importance of the supernatural ministry of the Spirit, insisting that Christians practice a morally strict lifestyle. He emphasized the second advent of Christ, apparently believing that this event would happen during his lifetime. Quickly gaining a substantial following, the movement spread throughout Asia Minor, North Africa, and Europe, reaching even to Rome.

The qualifying factor for ministry in the Church, according to Montanus, was possession of a spiritual gift rather than appointment to ecclesiastical office. He particularly emphasized the gift of prophecy and was soon joined by two prophetesses, Prisca and Maximilla. Speaking in tongues was probably also a common occurrence among the Montanists.[10] The Montanists preferred to be called *The New Prophecy* because they believed that God was renewing the prophetic ministry of the Church through them. Their opponents derisively referred to them as *Montanists* after the name of their leader and it is the name by which they became known.

The emphasis on spiritual gifts brought Montanus into sharp conflict with many church leaders who contended that the newly-developing ecclesiastical office held preeminence over any spiritual gift.[11] These leaders also took issue with the manner in which Montanus and his followers delivered their prophecies. Although they found no fault with the content of the prophecies, they accused them of delivering them in a frenzied state of ecstasy.[12] Declaring this to be proof of the demonic origin of the messages, the critics accused Montanus and his followers of being demon possessed.

Several regional councils or synods held in the latter half

of the second century censured Montanus and his followers. This calling of church councils, however, merely highlights the impact that Montanism was having throughout the Church. In their book, *Christian Initiation and Baptism in the Holy Spirit*, Kilian McDonnell and George Montague point out that these were the first councils in the history of the Church except for the Jerusalem council of Acts 15, and that "neither the threat of gnosticism, nor Marcionism had ever pressed the Church into calling councils."[13]

Support for Montanus and his followers was widespread. Eusebius indicates that Irenaeus was sent to Rome by the Gallic Christians to intercede on behalf of the Montanists.[14] His intercession initially induced the bishop of Rome to issue letters of peace to the Montanist churches, but later he withdrew them. Irenaeus must have been referring to the opposers of Montanus when he expressed his dismay at those who "set aside at once both the Gospel and the prophetic Spirit." These same men, said Irenaeus, could not admit the apostle Paul either, for in his epistle to the Corinthians "he expressly speaks of prophetical gifts, and recognizes men and women prophesying in the Church."[15]

In North Africa, the Montanists were defended by Tertullian who joined the movement around the year A.D. 200. In *Against Praxeas*, Tertullian says that the bishop of Rome initially "acknowledged the prophetic gifts of Montanus, Prisca, and Maximilla" and "bestowed his peace" upon the Montanist churches of Asia and Phrygia.[16] McDonnell points out that *peace* was a synonym for *personal and ecclesial communion*, and for the bishop to send letters of peace to the Montanist churches was to say, "We belong to the same communion, we celebrate the same Eucharist, we hold the same faith."[17]

A complication, however, arose through Praxeas who taught a doctrine called *monarchianism*, declaring that the Father,

Son, and Holy Spirit are one and the same. He successfully influenced the Roman bishop against the new prophets, and the letters of peace were withdrawn. Tertullian says that Praxeas did a twofold service for the devil at Rome. "He drove away prophecy and he brought in heresy; he put to flight the Paraclete, and he crucified the Father."[18] Tertullian also wrote seven books defending ecstatic prophecy, all of which were either lost or destroyed.[19]

After the death of Montanus, his followers became more strict in their asceticism, instituting fasts and placing more stringent demands upon all their adherents. By the onset of the third century, they also began to institutionalize, setting up their own ecclesiastical system with bishops and deacons. By 381, the Council at Constantinople finally declared that the Montanists should be regarded as pagans. In spite of this opposition, the movement continued at least into the fifth century when Augustine mentions their existence.

## Montanism: Heresy or Biblical Christianity?

One problem scholars face in evaluating Montanism is their dependence on the writings of the enemies of the Montanists, rather than on primary documents of the Montanists themselves. Writings, such as Tertullian's seven books on ecstatic prophecy, in which Montanists defended themselves, have not survived. They were either lost or destroyed by their enemies.

In spite of this, Montanism is slowly gaining a more favorable hearing. In 1750, for example, John Wesley read an early eighteenth century work by John Lacy called *The General Delusion of Christians Touching the Ways of God Revealing Himself To and By the Prophets*. It gives a positive view of Montanism, refuting many of the traditional accusations. After reading this book, Wesley wrote the following response in his *Journal* on August 15, 1750.

> I was fully convinced of what I had once suspected: (1) That the Montanists, in the second and third centuries, were real Scriptural Christians; and (2) That the grand reason why the miraculous gifts were so soon withdrawn, was not only that faith and holiness were well nigh lost, but that dry, formal, orthodox men began even then to ridicule whatever gifts they had not themselves, and to decry them all as either madness or imposture.[20]

Some detractors of Montanism contend that the movement represented an intrusion of pagan prophecy into second century Christianity.[21] No hard evidence is forthcoming to substantiate this claim, however. Such a claim "is completely false" according to David Aune in his extensive study of ancient prophecy, *Prophecy in the Early Church and the Ancient Mediterranean World*. He maintains that all major features of early Montanism, including the ecstatic nature of their prophetic utterances, "are derived from early Christianity."[22]

In summation, it is probably safe to say that Montanism was the first charismatic renewal within the Church and that it sought to bring revival to a rapidly hardening ecclesiasticism. The institutional church obviously overreacted to the movement and accelerated a trend of disregard and disdain toward spiritual gifts. It also began a trend, as Philip Schaff has pointed out, wherein a sharp line was drawn "between the age of the apostles, in which there had been direct supernatural revelations, and the later age, in which such revelations had disappeared."[23] McDonnell says, "The Church never really recovered its balance after it rejected Montanism."[24]

### The Final Touches
The threat of Montanism to the authority now invested in

the ecclesiastical office caused the Church to grant even more authority to the bishop thereby accelerating the process of institutionalization. Whereas the affairs of the first century Church were directed by a group of elders who were also called *bishops* or *overseers*,[25] the churches were now under the control of a single individual for whom the title *bishop* was reserved exclusively. Also at this time, the bishops began to be looked upon as the successors of the apostles. As such, they were perceived to be the possessors and guarantors of apostolic doctrine and they alone possessed the *charisma veritus*, the divine gift of knowledge from God giving them sole right to teach. By investing all authority in the office of the bishop, it was felt that the Church would be protected from heretical teachers.

This institutional trend brought a sharp division in the Church between clergy and laity, a division unknown in the New Testament Church. The criteria for teaching and leading ceased to be the calling or gifting of the Spirit, but was instead, ordination by ecclesiastical officials. Bultman points out that the gift of the Spirit to teach and lead "which was originally given by the Spirit to the person, is now understood as an office—charisma conveyed by ordination."[26] The clergy thus assumed all the ministerial responsibilities of the Church and a distinct priesthood parallel to that of the Old Testament emerged.[27]

The Church's reaction to Montanism contributed to the now rapid disappearance of spiritual gifts. By the third century, Origen would state explicitly that "these signs have diminished."[28] The freedom of the Spirit was being replaced by ceremonial ritual and ecclesiastical order. The final blow to the charismatic character of the Church would come with the conversion of Constantine and the Church's acquisition of earthly affluence and power.

## Notes

1 James L. Ash Jr., "The Decline of Ecstatic Prophecy in the Early Church," *Theological Studies* 37 (1976): 227.

2 See Gerald F. Hawthorne, *Philippians,* vol. 43 of *Word Biblical Commentary,* ed. David A. Hubbard and Glen W. Barker (Waco: TX: Word Books, 1983), 8.

3 Ignatius, "To the Trallians," *The Apostolic Fathers,* ed. Michael W. Holmes (Grand Rapids: Baker, 1992), 161.

4 Ignatius, "To the Smyrneans," *The Apostolic Fathers,* ed. Michael W. Holmes (Grand Rapids: Baker, 1992), 189.

5 Ash, "The Decline of Ecstatic Prophecy in the Early Church," 249.

6 Burnett Streeter, The Primitive Church (New York: MacMillan, 1929), 169-70.

7 Ash, *The Decline of Ecstatic Prophecy in the Early Church,* 228.

8 See Tertullian, "On Fasting," vol. 4 of *The Ante-Nicene Christian Library,* ed. Rev. Alexander Roberts and James Donaldson (1874; reprint, Grand Rapids: Eerdmans, 1972), 102, who says that the Montanists do not "overturn any rule of faith or hope." See Ronald E. Heine, *The Montanist Oracles and Testimonia* (Macon, GA: Mercer University Press, 1989), 27, who records the Montanist opponent, Epiphanius, as saying that the Montanists "accept all the Scriptures of the Old and New Testament, and likewise say that there is a resurrection of the dead." See also Philip Schaff, *Ante-Nicene Christianity,* vol. 2 of *History of the Christian Church,* (1910; reprint, Grand Rapids: Eerdmans, 1994), 421; and Hans von Campenhausen, *The Formation of the Christian Bible,* trans. J. A. Baker (Philadelphia: Fortress Press, 1972), 222.

9 John Lacy, *The General Delusion of Christians Touching the Ways of God's Revealing Himself To and By the Prophets* (1713, reprint; London: R. B. Seely and W. Burnside, 1832), 293. See also John Wesley, vol. 9 of *The Works of John Wesley,* 14 vols. (Grand Rapids: Zondervan, n.d.,), 485, who refers to Montanus as "not only a good man, but one of the best men then upon the earth."

10 This is the conviction of F. C. Klawiter, "The New Prophecy in Early Christianity: The Origin, Nature, and Development of Montanism, A.D. 165-200." Ph.D. diss., University of Chicago, 1975.

11 See Schaff, *History of the Christian Church* vol. 2, 424.

12 See Eusebius, 222 who has preserved fragments of the writings of Apollonius who makes this charge against the Montanists. Apollonius, nonetheless, recognizes spiritual gifts and declares that "the prophetic gift must remain in the whole Church until the final coming, even as the apostle insists." This clearly demonstrates that the conflict did not concern the le-

gitimacy of the gifts themselves but was, rather, a power struggle concerning the locus of authority in the Church.

[13] Kilian McDonnell and George Montague, *Christian Initiation and Baptism in the Holy Spirit* (Collegeville, MN: Liturgical, 1991), 108.

[14] Eusebius, 206. See also Schaff, vol. 2, 420, who says that Irenaeus was sent to Rome "to intercede on their [the Montanists] behalf." This same view is expressed by Grant, 136; McDonnell and Montague, 108; and David Wright, "Montanism: A Movement of Spiritual Renewal?" *Theological Renewal* (November 1982): 25.

[15] Irenaeus, *Against Heresies*, vol. 1 of *The Ante-Nicene Christian Library*, ed. Rev. Alexander Roberts and James Donaldson (1874; reprint, Grand Rapids: Eerdmans, 1972), 429. Irenaeus is referring specifically to the gospel of John. Some denied its validity and the validity of the prophetic gift; probably in reaction to the Montanists who derived much of their teaching concerning the Paraclete from this gospel. This is the view of Walter Bauer, *Orthodoxy and Heresy in Earliest Christianity*, eds. Robert A. Kraft and Gerhard Krodel (Philadelphia: Fortress Press, 1971), 141; W. H. C. Frend, *The Rise of Christianity* (Philadelphia: Fortress Press, 1984), 254; and Robert M. Grant, *Augustus to Constantine* (New York: Harper & Row, 1970), 136.

[16] Tertullian, *Against Praxeas*, vol. 3 of *Ante-Nicene Christian Library*, ed. Rev. Alexander Roberts and James Donaldson (1874; reprint, Grand Rapids: Eerdmans, 1972), 597.

[17] McDonnell and Montague, *Christian Initiation and the Baptism in the Holy Spirit*, 108.

[18] Tertullian, *Against Praxeas*, 597.

[19] Jerome, *Lives of Illustrious Men*, vol. 3 of *Nicene and Post-Nicene Fathers of the Christian Church*, 2nd Series, ed. Philip Schaff and Henry Wace (1892; reprint, Grand Rapids: Eerdmans, 1978.), 373.

[20] Nehemiah Curnack ed., vol. 3 of *The Journal of the Rev. John Wesley A.M.*, 8 vols. (London: Epworth, 1938), 490.

[21] Relying on the accounts of Montanism preserved by Eusebius and Epiphanius, modern scholars have often attempted to identify Montanism as representing an intrusion of the mystery religious cults of Asia Minor into second century Christianity. This began with Augustus Neander, *General History of the Christian Religion and Church*, vol. 1 of 4 vols., trans. Joseph Torrey (Boston: Houghton, Mifflin & Co., 1871), 513, who says "We cannot be surprised to find the Phrygian temperament which displayed itself in the ecstasies of Cybele and Baachus, exhibiting itself once more in the ecstasies and somnambulisms of the Montanists." See, however, Walter Bauer, *Orthodoxy and Heresy in Earliest Christianity*, eds. Robert A. Kraft and Gerhard Krodel (Philadelphia: Fortress Press, 1971), 141, who notes the

obvious biased reporting of both Eusebius and Epiphanius and says that their accounts are "hardly anything more than abusive satires" and insists that "one should reject as biased all of the judgments found in these words even if they are delivered in the costume of historical narrative."

[22] David Aune, *Prophecy in Early Christianity and the Ancient Mediterranean World* (Grand Rapids: Eerdmans, 1983), 313.

[23] Philip Schaff and Henry Wace ed., *Nicene and Post-Nicene Fathers of the Christian Church*, 2nd Series (Grand Rapids: Eerdmans, 1978), 231.

[24] Kilian McDonnell, *The Baptism in the Holy Spirit* (Notre Dame: Charismatic Renewal Services, 1972), 44.

[25] This seems to have been the normal pattern in the churches Paul established although James seems to have functioned in a capacity of first among equals in the oversight of the church in Jerusalem.

[26] Bultman, *New Testament Theology*, 2: 52.

[27] See Cyprian, *Letters*, vol. 51 of *The Fathers of the Church*, who in his attempt to thwart widespread schisms in the Church makes repeated parallels of the authority of the bishop with that of the Old Testament priesthood. See also Peter Hinchliff, *Cyprian of Carthage* (Great Britain: Geoffrey Chapman, 1974), 103, who points out Cyprian's application of Old Testament texts to the bishop's office and his transference of passages referring to the Old Testament Levitical priesthood to the Christian ministry.

[28] Origen, *Against Celsus*, 614.

CHAPTER 5

# The Impact of Constantine's Conversion on the Charismatic Character of the Church

### Merger of Church and State

THE CONVERSION OF CONSTANTINE in A.D. 312 marked the beginning of the Church's rise to earthly power and the end of the *charismata* as part of its life and ministry. In A.D. 313, Constantine issued the *Edict of Milan*, a decree not only permitting freedom of worship to all inhabitants of the empire, but also granting special favors to the Church. As a result, the churches began to be frequented by those seeking the political and social advantages that identifying with the Church now offered.

Constantine became directly involved in the affairs of the Church thereby setting the stage for the amalgamation of the powers of the Church and state. In A.D. 325, for example, he called the first General Council of the Christian Church. Bishops from all parts of the empire convened in Nicea, a city in Asia Minor, at government expense. Constantine himself presided over the first session, and in later sessions, he intervened at significant points in the discussions even though he had not yet been baptized.

Constantine also initiated the building of facilities to accommodate the religious gatherings of Christians. Prior to this, believers had met primarily in homes. Constantine, however, erected buildings in which the Church was to meet. These he modeled after the architecture of the civic auditoriums of the day. This architecture, with its elevated throne-like seating at the front for the bishop and its rows of seating for the congregation, made significant congregational involvement impractical. In addtion, the liturgy and worship style, once plain and personal, were now adorned with the pomp and practice of the Imperial court.[1]

## The Exclusive Religion of the State

Constantine died in A.D. 337, but his sons continued and expanded his policy of favoring the Christian Church. In A.D. 381, the new emperor, Theodosius I, made Christianity the exclusive religion of the state. Any who dared subscribe to any other form of worship, in fact, risked punishment from the state.[2] As a result, hordes of unconverted pagans filled the churches, bringing with them heathen ideas and practices. Moral laxity, already having fractured the pristine nature of the Church, now dominated much of her life. One who mourned this appalling state of affairs was John Chrysostom (A.D. 347-407), patriarch of Constantinople. He complained that the character of the Church of his day was no different from that of the marketplace or theater.

> If anyone is trying or intending to corrupt a woman, there is no place, I suppose, that seems to him more suitable than the Church. And if anything to be sold or bought, the Church appears more convenient than the market. Or if any wish to say or to hear any scandal, you will find that this to be had here more than the forum without.[3]

This being the case, it is perhaps not surprising that Chrysostom expresses an ignorance of the *charismata* listed in 1

Corinthians 12. He says, "The obscurity is produced by our ignorance of the facts referred to and their cessation."[4] In his region at least, spiritual gifts had apparently ceased to operate. The reason seems obvious.

## Adoption of the Roman Political Model

The elevation of Christianity to official status as the religion of the empire brought a political cohesion to the Church it had previously not known. A universal system of church government began to emerge, and it soon became clear that it reflected the prevailing political pattern of the Roman Empire. At the same time, the bishop of the city of Rome began to be looked upon as a first among equals. With his claim as head over the Church founded by Peter and Paul, he garnered increasing influence for himself, and in so doing, he paved the way for the papacy to be the spiritual counterpart of the political head-of-state, the Roman emperor. Because of these developments, Rudolph Sohm notes, "The constitution of the Church was in the main modeled on the organization of the Empire."[5]

These trends also brought a solidification of a doctrine of *sacramentalism.* The ordinances of baptism and the Lord's Supper began to be looked upon as *sacraments* possessing inherent salvific value and able to impart the grace and gifts of God.[6] Furthermore, only the bishop or his appointed representative had the right to administer these sacraments. In fact, involvement by an *unordained* person in their administration rendered them ineffective.

These developments had devastating ramifications for the ministry of the Holy Spirit through the people of God. The gifts which once had flowed spontaneously among the whole congregation were now bound to the ecclesiastical office and transmitted by a sacramental act. In the New Testament Church, the people had been participants in spontaneous worship, but they now became passive spectators in a highly developed sacramental ritual presided over by ecclesiastical officials.

## Emergence of Doctrinal Strife

The Church's rise to power also marked the beginning of many fierce doctrinal battles. Free from the threat of persecution and enjoying the favor of the emperor, the Church now gave its attention to theological questions which usually became litmus tests of one's orthodoxy. Many violent struggles ensued producing sharp divisions in the Church. Basil of Caesarea, bishop of Cappadocia (A.D. 370-379), likened it to a great naval battle being fought by men who "cherish a deadly hate against one another."[7]

> But what storm at sea was ever so wild and fierce as this tempest of the churches. In it every landmark of the Fathers has been moved; every foundation, every bulwark of opinion has been shaken; everything buoyed up on the unsound is dashed about and shaken down. We attack one another. If our enemy is not the first to strike us, we are wounded by the comrade at our side.[8]

In such a state, it is not surprising that the spiritual gifts, which Paul taught were to function within the context of Christian love, became extinct in the institutional church. The Church's rise to earthly affluence and power marked the end of the *charismata* as a vital part of its corporate life and ministry. A. J. Gordon, Baptist pastor and founder of Gordon College in Boston, was correct when he said,

> It is not altogether strange that when the Church forgot her citizenship in heaven and began to establish herself

in luxury and splendor on earth, she should cease to exhibit the supernatural gifts of heaven.[9]

Nonetheless, although disappearing from the ecclesiastical church, the gifts did not disappear altogether. They now began to appear among the believers who, in an effort to escape the corruption which they perceived to have taken over both the Church and the world, withdrew from society in order to live lives of prayer and devotion to God. Known as *monastics*, they became a vital force during the Middle Ages and preserved the miraculous dimension of the Christian faith.

---

### Notes

[1] See Eusebius, 393-94 for a description of one of these cathedrals. See also Justo Gonzales, vol. 1 of *A History of Christian Thought*, 3 vols. (Nashville: Abingdon, 1987), 261-65.

[2] Earle E. Cairns, *Christianity Through the Centuries* (Grand Rapids: Zondervan, 1981), 124.

[3] Chrysostom, *Homilies on First Corinthians* vol. 12 of *Nicene and Post-Nicene Fathers of the Christian Church*, 2nd Series, ed. Philip Schaff and Henry Wace (Grand Rapids: Eerdmans, 1978), 221.

[4] Chrysostom, *Homilies on First Corinthians*, 168.

[5] Rudolph Sohm, *Outlines of Church History*, (London: MacMillan, 1913), 47.

[6] That the earliest Christians were not sacramentalists is borne out by Irenaeus, *Fragments From the Lost Writings of Irenaeus*, vol. 1 of *The Ante-Nicene Christian Library*, ed. Rev. Alexander Roberts and James Donaldson (Edinburgh: T & T Clark, 1874), 570, where Irenaeus tells of certain slaves of recent Christian converts being arrested and "imagining" communion to be the "actual" blood and body of Christ testified as such before the inquisitors. The authorites then sought through torture to force two martyrs to confess it was so but they refused to confess the mistaken view of the slaves.

[7] Basil, *On the Spirit*, vol. 7 of *Nicene and Post-Nicene Fathers of the Christian Church*, 2nd Series, ed. Philip Schaff and Henry Wace (Grand Rapids: Eerdmans, 1978), 48.

[8] Basil, *On the Spirit*, 49.

[9] A. J. Gordon, *The Ministry of Healing* (Harrisburg: Christian Publ., 1961), 64.

# CHAPTER 6

# Monasticism:
# The Rise of Another
# Charismatic Movement

THE MONASTICS were devout believers who lived ascetic lives in an effort to experience the presence and power of God in a very personal manner. The initial stage of the movement was individualistic with these ascetics living as hermits. Around A.D. 320, they began to gather together in communities where they lived a totally self-sufficient lifestyle. During the Middle Ages (A.D. 600-1517), these communities or *monasteries*, as they were called, became centers of learning and the monks served as custodians of books and manuscripts. In complete devotion to God, they gave themselves to study, prayer, and meditation. Indeed, they proved to be shining lights during the period of intense social decadence known as the Dark Ages (c.a. 500-1300).

Following Constantine's ascent to power, most supernatural phenomena are recorded either by monastics or by those who venerated the monastic lifestyle. Cardinal Leon Joseph Suenens is correct in saying, "In its beginnings, monasticism was, in fact, a charismatic movement."[1] The miraculous gifts of the Holy Spirit, which disappeared from the institutional church, now appeared among the monastics. Many monks gained notoriety for their power in prayer and their ability to produce healing, deliverance from demonic oppression, and other miraculous phenomena. Church fathers, such as Athanasius, Augustine, and Jerome, who speak of miracles, either practiced the monastic lifestyle themselves or were closely associated with those who did.

## Antony

Antony (A.D. 251-356) is usually considered the founder of monasticism. He was reared in an affluent Christian home in Egypt. Soon after his parents' deaths when Antony was about eighteen years old, he felt that God directed him to give up his possessions and live a life of absolute devotion. After selling his parents' three-hundred-acre estate, he retired to a cave in the desert, and there he spent his time in prayer and meditation.

Antony's fame for holiness and for power in prayer eventually spread throughout the empire. Imitating his way of life, many others adopted the hermit lifestyle. Others, inspired by Antony's devotion, organized themselves into monastic communities.

*The Life of Antony*, written by the bishop, Athanasius, is filled with accounts of the supernatural. According to Athanasius, many people from all walks of life visited Antony in the desert seeking his prayers and wisdom. He is said to have possessed the gift of discerning of Spirits and often knew things supernaturally. His prayers brought healing to the sick and deliverance to the demonized. Athanasius speaks of one particular occasion when many gathered at the entrance of Antony's cave seeking his prayers. Antony finally emerged and "through him the Lord healed the bodily ailments of many present, and cleansed others from evil spirits."[2]

Antony lived until his 105th year. According to Athanasius, he remained physically strong to the end. His eyes were undimmed and he retained all of his teeth. Shortly before his death, he visited the other monks in the desert and shared with them that it would be the last time they would see him. They responded with tears and embraces, and he, in turn, joyously exhorted them to continue in their devotion to God. Shortly thereafter, having given directions concerning the distribution of his few meager possessions, he pulled his feet under him (like Jacob, Gen. 49:33) and died with an expression of joy on his face.

### Pachomius

Pachomius (A.D. 292-346), a discharged soldier, was probably inspired by the life of Antony to live for a time as a hermit. One day while he was sitting in his cell, an angel appeared to him, saying, "Go and gather together unto thyself those who are wandering, and be thou dwelling with them, and lay down for them such laws as I shall tell unto thee."[3] Subsequently, Pachomius organized the first monastery about A.D. 320 at Tabennisi on the east bank of the Nile. Each member of the community had a work assignment, a scheduled time of worship, and clothing similar to his fellow monks. In addition to private devotional time, they had scheduled times of corporate worship.

One ancient writer described Pachomius as "a man endowed with apostolic grace both in teaching and in performing miracles."[4] On one occasion, he had a visitor from the west who spoke Latin, a language Pachomius did not know. After three hours of earnest prayer, however, Pachomius was enabled to converse with the visitor in Latin. It was reported that on several occasions when the need arose, Pachomius was enabled to speak in a language he had not learned. This indicates that speaking in tongues was probably not uncommon in the monastic communities.

## Athanasius

Athanasius (A. D. 295-373), known as *The Father of Ortho-doxy*, was bishop of Alexandria in Egypt. His life actually spanned both sides of the Council of Nicea. He is best known for his writings against Arianism. Arius taught that Christ was a created being who was different from and less than the Father. This teaching gained many followers in the fourth century.

Athanasius, on the other hand, insisted that Christ was coequal, coeternal, and consubstantial with the Father. For these views he suffered exile five times, but his teaching was finally accepted as the official doctrine of the Church.

Athanasius was obviously familiar with the supernatural ministry of the Holy Spirit. He wrote an account of the life of his friend Antony, recording the many miracles associated with his life. Athanasius concluded his account of Antony, saying,

> And we ought not to doubt whether such marvels were wrought by the hand of a man. For it is the promise of the Saviour, when He saith, "If ye have faith as a grain of mustard seed, ye shall say to this mountain, remove hence and it shall remove, and nothing shall be impossible unto you."[5]

By the time of Athanasius, the office of bishop had already become surrounded by so many political trappings that many considered the position to be an occasion to sin. Athanasius, however, argued against this notion in a letter to a friend, Dracontius, who felt he must choose between a monastic life-style committed to God or that of a bishop surrounded by ease and temptation. Athanasius communicates to Dracontius that he can live the kind of devoted life his soul desires even as a bishop. He tells Dracontius that he knows bishops who fast and monks who do not, and of bishops who have not married and monks who have married and produced children. He also says, "We know bishops who work wonders [miracles] and monks who do not."[6]

Athanasius' testimony clearly indicates his familiarity with and openness to the miraculous gifts of the Spirit. His writings reveal no knowledge of a theory that these gifts were to cease, nor that they were reserved for a select, saintly few.

### Hilarion

Hilarion (A.D. 305-385) was born in the city of Gaza in Palestine to pagan parents who provided him with a good education. At an early age, he became a believer in Jesus Christ and from the beginning, exhibited a tendency toward an ascetic lifestyle.

While still in his teens, Hilarion heard of the fame of Antony and visited him at his desert retreat in Egypt. As a result of this visit, Hilarion dedicated himself to live a life of devotion in the wilderness of Palestine. He, like Antony, gained a reputation for holiness and power in prayer. Jerome, who knew him personally, says, "Time would fail me if I wished to relate all the miracles which were wrought by him."[7]

On one occasion, Hilarion found a paralyzed man lying near the entrance of his abode. He inquired about the man's identity, and then,

> weeping much and stretching out his hand to the prostrate man he said, "I bid you in the name of our Lord Jesus Christ, arise and walk." The words were still on the lips of the speaker, when, with miraculous speed, the limbs were strengthened and the man arose and stood firm.[8]

Hilarion spent the last few years of his life in Cyprus, and there he died. A friend and admirer later stole his body and returned it to Palestine. According to Jerome, who was writing after Hilarion's death, miracles continued both at the site of his death in Cyprus as well as at his tomb in Palestine.

## Ambrose

Ambrose (A.D. 340-397) became bishop of Milan in A.D. 374, having given up a successful political career to do so. He was both an able administrator and a very effective preacher. In fact, his preaching was instrumental in bringing Augustine to the knowledge of the truth, and in A.D. 387, he baptized Augustine.

On one occasion in Milan, reports Augustine, a vast throng gathered at the tomb of two martyrs. In a dream, the location of the hidden remains of these martyrs had been revealed to Ambrose. As the crowd gathered, a blind man miraculously received his sight.[9]

Although he lived and ministered during a time of spiritual decline, Ambrose, in his writings, expresses an awareness of and openness to the supernatural manifestations of the Spirit. This perspective is clear in his work, *Of the Holy Spirit*, in which he attempts to demonstrate the unity of the Trinity by showing that what can be said of the Father and Son may also be said of the Spirit.

> You see the Father and Christ also set teachers in the churches; and as the Father gives the gift of healings, so too does the Son give; as the Father gives the gift of tongues, so too has the Son also granted it. In like manner we have heard also above concerning the Holy Spirit that He too grants the same kinds of graces. So,

then, the Spirit gives the same gifts as the Father, and the Son also gives them.[10]

This passage expresses a clear acceptance of charismatic phenomena such as healing and speaking in tongues. It should also be noted that he speaks of these gifts in the present tense, indicating that he believed them to be valid in the Church of his day.

### Jerome

Jerome (A.D. 347-420) became a Christian in A.D. 360 and for several years afterwards was a wandering student in Rome and the cities of Gaul. He became an astute scholar and a lover of classical learning. While traveling through the Orient, and in Antioch, he became critically ill. During this sickness, Christ appeared to him and reproached him for his devotion to classical study. Repenting, he turned, became a diligent Bible student, studied Hebrew, and lived as a hermit not far from Antioch. One writer has called Jerome "the ablest scholar the ancient Western Church could boast."[11]

Later, Jerome moved to Palestine where he became the head of a monastery. During this time in Palestine, until his death in A.D. 420, Jerome produced the works for which he is remembered, including his greatest work, the Latin translation of the Scriptures, *The Vulgate*. From the Council of Trent (1545-63) until recently, this was the only official Bible of the Roman Catholic Church.

Jerome quite obviously believed in the supernatural ministry of the Holy Spirit. The miraculous is often mentioned by him, especially in his work *The Life of Saint Hilarion*. Perhaps the most outstanding miracle recorded by Jerome is of Hilarion stilling a raging sea embroiled by a violent earthquake.

According to Jerome, the huge wall of water that was about to destroy the village of Epidaurus became still and calm before the outstretched hands of Hilarion. Jerome then remarks,

> Verily, what was said to the Apostles, "If ye have faith, ye shall say unto this mountain, Remove into the sea, and it shall be done," may even be literally fulfilled if one has such faith as the Lord commanded the Apostles to have.[12]

Jerome lived well into the fifth century. He gives no hint in his writings that he expected miracles to cease. Like Athanasius, he indicates that miracles are within the grasp of all who will believe according to the words of Jesus.

## Augustine

Augustine (A.D. 354-430), after his conversion in A.D. 387, became the bishop of Hippo in North Africa. He became an influential thinker and a voluminous writer. He is often acclaimed as the greatest of the church fathers. In fact, much theology of both Catholicism and Protestantism is rooted in his thought.[13]

Early in his Christian experience, Augustine seems to have looked askance at the miraculous ministry of the Holy Spirit. In his homily *The Epistle of Saint John,* he referred to the tongues at Pentecost as a sign "adapted to the time" which had passed away.[14] He then goes on to make his point that the witness of the Holy Spirit's presence is no longer given by miracles, but by the love of God in one's heart for the Church.

Later in life, however, Augustine shows great interest in the supernatural and relates many miraculous incidents in his own life and in the lives of others. In his work *The City of God,* one chapter is entitled "Concerning Miracles Which

Were Wrought in Order That the World Might Believe in Christ and Which Cease Not to be Wrought now That the World Does Believe." Augustine says, "For even now, miracles are wrought in the name of Christ, whether by His sacraments or by prayer or the relics of His saints."[15]

Augustine then proceeds to describe various miracles of which he is personally aware. These include healings from blindness, cancer, gout, hemorrhoids, demon possession, and even the raising of the dead. Some were healed as a result of a simple prayer, and a paralytic was healed at the moment of his baptism. Miracles were obviously not uncommon in his area, for he says, "I am so pressed by the promise of finishing this work that I cannot record all the miracles I know."[16]

Augustine also discusses a phenomena which he called *jubilation* which is very similar to what modern Charismatics would call "singing in the Spirit," that is, in other tongues. According to Augustine, a person begins to jubilate when the mouth is not able to express with words what the heart is singing. The person continues to make sounds, but the sounds are inarticulate because the heart is giving utterance to what it cannot say in words. He then says,

> And for whom is such jubilation fitting if not for the ineffable God? For he is ineffable whom one cannot express in words; and if you cannot express him in words, and yet you cannot remain silent either, then what is left but to sing in jubilation, so that your heart may rejoice without words, and your unbounded joy may not be confined by the limits of syllables.[17]

Augustine's interest in the miraculous has led some writers to conclude correctly that, in later life, he changed his views on the miraculous ministry of the Holy Spirit.[18] Nevertheless, the die was cast and influential leaders chose to adopt his earlier statements; thus, they spread throughout the Church and down through the ages as representative of his position. Augustine may, therefore, be responsible, more than anyone else, for what has become known as the *Cessation Theory.*

## Benedict

As a teenager, Benedict of Nursia (ca. A.D. 480-547) was sent by his parents to Rome to obtain a good education. About A.D. 500, shocked by the vice of that city, he retired to a cave in the mountains east of Rome where he lived as a hermit. In about A.D. 529, he founded the monastery of Monte Cassino, a landmark that survived until World War II when it was destroyed by bombardment.

Another of Benedict's lasting contributions was what became known as *The Rule of Benedict.* It provided an organizational pattern for life, work, and worship in communal monastic life. It became one of the most important plans for monastic life in the Middle Ages throughout Europe.

Benedict gained renown for both his power in prayer and in facilitating miracles. The story is told of how, on one occasion, a monastery wall under construction collapsed, killing one of the monks. Benedict ordered the mangled body to be brought to his room. Having closed the door, he knelt down and prayed earnestly. Within one hour, to everyone's astonishment, the young man revived and returned to his work on the wall.[19]

Benedict did not confine his ministry to the members of his monastery. He reached out to the people beyond the walls. "He cured their sick, relieved the distress, and is said to have raised the dead on more than one occasion."[20] In his *Dialogues*, Gregory relates incidents in which Benedict cast evil spirits out of certain individuals. On one occasion, an evil spirit entered one of the monks and threw him to the ground in a violent convulsion. When Benedict saw what was happening, he struck the man on the cheek. The evil spirit immediately left and never returned.[21]

Benedict was also endowed with the revelation gifts of the Holy Spirit and the gift of prophecy. He often described to his colleagues what they had done in his absence. In addition, he foretold future events. He was forewarned of his own death and bade his disciples to dig his grave six days before the end. He died standing in the chapel with his hands raised toward heaven.[22]

### Gregory the Great

Gregory the Great (A.D 540-604) was born of wealthy parents and received a good education. About A.D 570 he became prefect of Rome, a position of significant honor. After his father died, Gregory surrendered his fortune and entered a Benedictine monastery. There he gained recognition as a gifted leader, and subsequently, when Pope Pelagius died in A.D 590, Gregory was elected to succeed him..

In his *Dialogues*, Gregory records many miracles of which he has personal knowledge, including the raising of the dead. Many of these miracles reflect Mark 11:23 where Jesus said, "If anyone says to this mountain, 'Go throw yourself into the sea,' and does not doubt in his heart but believes what he says will happen, it will be done for him." For example, Gregory tells of Bishop Boniface whose garden suffered an invasion of caterpillars.

> Seeing all his vegetables going to ruin, he turned to the caterpillars and said, 'I adjure you in the Name of our Lord Jesus Christ, depart from here and stop eating these vegetables.' In obedience to his voice all the

51

caterpillars, down to the very last one, disappeared from the garden.[23]

Gregory also tells of a boy who, while drawing water from the river, fell in and was being swept away by the current. Benedict, the abbott (leader) of the nearby monastery, aware of the crisis through a word of knowledge, charged Brother Maurus to hurry to the river to rescue the boy. Running to the river's edge, Maurus spotted the frantic boy being swept downstream, and without realizing it, he continued to run on the water until he reached the boy. Grabbing him by the hair, he dragged him to safety on the riverbank. Benedict would take no credit for the miracle but attributed it to the obedience of his disciple. Maurus, however, claimed that the rescue was "due entirely to his abbott's command."[24]

Gregory also tells of a man named Marcellus being raised from the dead. Marcellus died on Saturday and because he could not be buried the same day, his sisters sought the prayers of Fortunatus, the bishop of that area. Fortunatus went to the home of the deceased early Sunday morning and, kneeling near the corpse, began to pray. After praying for some time, he arose and sat down. Then in a subdued voice, he called "Brother Marcellus." Marcellus opened his eyes, looked at Fortunatus and said, "What have you done? What have you done?" Fortunatus then asked, "What have I done?" Marcellus explained how, on the previous day, two people [angels] had come to escort him to the abode of the blessed. A messenger had intervened, however, commanding, "Take him back because Bishop Fortunatus is visiting his home." Marcellus revived, quickly regained his strength, and lived for years after this miracle.[25]

Gregory obviously believed in miracles, and he believed that miracles were to continue throughout the history of the

Church since he nowhere speaks of a theory of cessation. He does emphasize that it was *holy* men of God who performed these miracles, thereby exhibiting the medieval tendency to associate miracles with the ascetic and *saintly* lifestyle. This undue regard for the ascetic life actually divided the Church during this period.

## Conclusion

During the Middle Ages, miracles became associated exclusively with the monastic lifestyle. In the apostolic Church, the *charismata* were available to all believers that all might benefit. In the medieval church, however, these miraculous gifts became the sole possession of those mystical *saints* who had withdrawn from the world and society.

---

## Notes

[1] Leon Joseph Cardinal Suenens, *A New Pentecost?* (New York: Seabury, 1975), 38.

[2] Athanasius, *Life of Antony*, vol. 4 of *Nicene and Post-Nicene Fathers of the Christian Church*, 2nd Series, ed. Philip Schaff and Henry Wace (Grand Rapids: Eerdmans, 1978), 200.

[3] Ann Freemantle, *A Treasury of Early Christianity* (New York: New American Library, 1953), 389.

[4] Jerome and Gennadius, *Illustrious Men of the Church,* vol. 3 of *Nicene and Post-Nicene Fathers of the Christian Church*, 2nd Series, ed. Philip Schaff and Henry Wace (Grand Rapids: Eerdmans, 1978), 387.

[5] Athanasius, *Life of Anthony*, 218.

[6] Athanasius, *Letters of Athanasius* vol. 4 of *Nicene and Post-Nicene Fathers of the Christian Church*, 2nd Series, ed. Philip Schaff and Henry Wace (Grand Rapids: Eerdmans, 1978), 560

[7] Jerome, *The Life of Saint Hilarion* vol. 6 of *Nicene and Post-Nicene Fathers of the Christian Church*, 2nd Series, ed. Philip Schaff and Henry Wace (Grand Rapids: Eerdmans, 1978), 309

[8] Jerome, *The Life of Saint Hilarion*, 314.

[9] Augustine, *The City of God*, vol. 2 of *Nicene and Post-Nicene Fathers of the Christian Church*, 1st Series, ed. Philip Schaff and Henry Wace (Grand Rapids: Eerdmans, 1979), 485.

[10] Ambrose, *Of the Spirit* vol. 10 of *Nicene and Post-Nicene Fathers of the Christian Church*, 2nd Series, ed. Philip Schaff and Henry Wace (Grand Rapids: Eerdmans, 1978), 134.

[11] Williston Walker, *A History of the Christian Church* (New York: Charles Scribner, 1920), 173.

[12] Jerome, *The Life of Saint Hilarion*, 313.

[13] Cairns, *Christianity Through the Centuries*, 146.

[14] Augustine, *The Epistle of Saint John*, vol. 12 of *Nicene and Post-Nicene Fathers of the Christian Church*, 1st Series, ed. Philip Schaff and Henry Wace (Grand Rapids: Eerdmans, 1978), 497-498.

[15] Augustine, *The City of God*, 485.

[16] Augustine, *The City of God*, 489.

[17] Francis Sullivan, *Charism and Charismatic Renewal* (Dublin: Gill and MacMillan, 1982), 147; See also Eddie Ensley, *Sounds of Wonder* (New York: Paulist Press, 1977).

[18] See Richard Chenevix Trench, *Notes on the Miracles of Our Lord* (New York: Revell, n.d.), 44 who discusses Augustine's varied views concerning the continuance of miracles in the Church.

[19] Saint Gregory the Great, *Dialogues*, vol. 39 of *The Fathers of the Church*, trans. Odo John Zimmerman (New York: Fathers of the Church, 1959), 76-77.

[20] Michael Walsh ed., *Butler's Lives of the Saints* (San Francisco: Harper, 1991), 212.

[21] Gregory, *Dialogues*, 98.

[22] Walsh, *Butler's Lives of the Saints*, 212.

[23] Gregory, *Dialogues*, 39.

[24] Gregory, *Dialogues*, 69.

[25] Gregory, *Dialogues*, 48-49.

CHAPTER 7

# Developments Within Monasticism and the Ecclesiastical Church

DURING THE MIDDLE AGES, the transformation of the old apostolic Church into the medieval Roman Catholic Church was fully consummated. The papal office became fully developed and popes exercised civil as well as spiritual power. They collected taxes, raised armies, and subjugated kings and rulers. The ecclesiastical church thus became the dominant force in society and spread its influence throughout the western world.

This preoccupation with earthly affluence and political power produced a dearth of spiritual gifts in the institutional church. Illustrating this fact is a story about Thomas Aquinas visiting Rome and being shown the church's wealth by Pope Innocent IV. In the course of their observations, Innocent said to Aquinas, "You see that the Church is no longer in an age in which she can say, 'Silver and gold have I none.'" Aquinas replied, "It is true, nor can she say to the lame man, 'Rise up and walk.'"[1]

During this same period, monasticism continued to be the arena in which spiritual gifts found freedom of expression. By 600, however, monasticism itself was losing much of its spiritual life and vitality. The ascetic lifestyle, which had emerged from a desire for the immediate presence of Christ, gradually drifted into much legalism and spiritual pride. As the monas-

55

teries became wealthy through community thrift and owner-ship, laziness, avarice, and gluttony also crept in.[2]

As the moral fiber of monasticism wore thin, exaggerated miraculous phenomena were increasingly reported. Not only did legendary folklore become entangled with historical real-ity, but also it was not uncommon for routine events to be reported in terms of heroic feats of faith. Reports of levita-tion, apparitions, flying through the air, and other bizarre events were all too typical of this era of monastic life.

In the seventeenth century, Jean Bolland organized a group of his fellow Jesuits into a society for the express pur-pose of doing a critical study and publication of the lives of the saints. Their work resulted in a pruning of the legends and exaggerations that had grown up and entangled themselves with historical reality. Cardinal Suenens, himself a charis-matic, says that we can thank heaven "and the Bollandists" for their careful pruning.[3]

## The Legend of St. Brandon

An example of such reports is the tale of the Irish saint, Brandon, who is said to have discovered an island in the At-lantic on which there was a monastery. As the story goes, at the island monastery, Brandon had discovered twenty-four Irish monks who had lived miraculously for eighty years on the island. During all this time, they had been miraculously served twelve loaves of bread daily, except on Sunday when the portion doubled. In addition, none had ever been sick. They wore royal robes made of golden cloth and moved about in procession. They celebrated mass with lighted can-dles and conducted evensong. Apparently having taken a vow of silence, they had never spoken a word to one another in all those eighty years.[4]

## Mysticism and Superstition

An air of superstition thus surrounds many of the miracles of this period. It was not uncommon for them to be associated with the bones and relics of saints, with shrines, and with prayers offered to saints and the virgin Mary. Schaff describes a typical monastery of this era as a place consumed with a sort of superstitious awareness of the spirit world. He says,

> The miraculous belonged to the monk's daily food. He was surrounded by spirits. Visions and revelations occurred by day and night. Single devils and devils in bands were roaming about at all hours in the cloistral spaces, in the air and on foot, to deceive the unwary and to shake the faith of the vigilant.[5]

In spite of this, the possible existence of the genuine should not be dismissed simply because of the abundance of the counterfeit. It should be remembered that legends often have a base of truth and reality from which they are derived. In addition, the possibility of psychic and demonically inspired phenomena being mistaken for acts of God should also be considered. In conclusion, there is no reason to suppose that many authentic miracles actually occurred, for, as in every era, there were devout believers.

## Miracles and Missionary Expansion

Some of the more credible miracles of this period seem to be associated with the missionary expansion of the Church. Ansgar (A.D. 800-865), for example, called *The Apostle of the North*, was one of the first missionaries to Scandinavia. Described as a mystic "moved by visions and dreams," he is said to have experienced visions from God even as a child.[6] When extolled by his contemporaries for the performance of numerous miracles, Ansgar said that the greatest miracle would be if God ever made a thoroughly pious man out of him.[7]

Miracles also accompanied the arrival of the gospel to Great Britain in the late sixth and early seventh centuries. Augustine, for example, arrived on the island around 597, having been sent by Pope Gregory. Reporting on Augustine's mission in his *Ecclesiastical History of the English Nation,* the Venerable Bede (A.D. 673-735) tells of a letter written by Gregory around 601 in which he commends Augustine because "the English by outward miracles are drawn to inward grace."[8] The miracles must have been numerous, for Gregory, acknowledging that Augustine has obviously received "the gift of working miracles," cautions Augustine not to be "puffed up by the number of them."[9]

## Saints or Sorcerers?

During the Middle Ages, a sharp distinction arose between those who performed miracles and those who did not. The Church maintained a strong bias against the occurrence of miracles among the common people. This bias was clearly demonstrated by the Roman Church's publication of the *Roman Ritual* around the year A.D. 1000. It declared, among other things, that speaking in tongues among the common people was to be considered *prima facie* evidence of demon possession. Among the monastics and Church hierarchy, however, it could be considered evidence of sainthood! Miracles became associated exclusively with the ascetic lifestyle and any occurrence of miracles among the common people was looked upon as the work of sorcery or witchcraft. Since the reading of the Scriptures by the common people in their own language was discouraged, this left the masses at the mercy of a highly complex and elaborate religious system that offered corporate identity but no personal access to God.

## Notes

[1] Adam Clarke, *The New Testament of Our Lord and Savior Jesus Christ with a Commentary and Critical Notes* (New York: Nelson and Phillips, n.d.), 705.

[2] Cairns, *Christianity Through the Centuries*, 155.

[3] Suenens, *A New Pentecost?* 39.

[4] Schaff, vol. 5, 319.

[5] Schaff, vol. 5, 317.

[6] Ruth A. Tucker, *From Jerusalem to Irian Jaya* (Grand Rapids: Zondervan, 1983), 49.

[7] Schaff, vol. 5, 113-115.

[8] Bede, *Bede's Ecclesiastical History of the English Nation* (London: J.M. Dent & Sons, 1963), 54.

[9] Bede, 54.

# CHAPTER 8

# Monastic Renewal

A RESURGENCE OF GENUINE spiritual renewal began in the eleventh century. It breathed new life into the Church at large, and into the monastic movement in particular. New orders including the Cistercians, the Franciscans, and the Dominicans emerged. Whereas the earlier monastic orders had cloistered themselves from the world, these newer orders, especially the Franciscans and the Dominicans, went among the people. Known as *preaching friars*, they preached the Gospel in the language of the people and helped them in various ways.

An outstanding trait of these preaching friars was their commitment to obey literally all the commands of Jesus. Motivated by devotion, they took vows of poverty, chastity, and obedience. They emulated Jesus' disciples (Lk. 10:1-12) who were to go on preaching missions without carrying extra money or clothing, thus putting themselves in a position of dependence on God and at the mercy of the people. In addition, they could not help but see Jesus' instructions and promises regarding miracles. This facilitated the manifestation of biblical miracles in their own lives and ministries.

These preaching friars thus restored to the Church a much-needed dimension. By adhering to the words of Jesus, they recovered the purity and faith of an earlier day. This devotion and expectation facilitated what may be considered another charismatic renewal at a crucial point in the history of the Church.

## Bernard of Clairvaux

Bernard (1090-1153) was born of noble parentage in Fon-
taines, Burgundy, in what is now east-central France. Although he had the opportunity to pursue a secular education,
his desire for the contemplative life prompted him to enter
the monastery at Citeaux in 1112. Having made remarkable
progress, after three years he was commissioned by the abbot
of Citeaux to establish a new monastery at Clairvaux in 1115.

From Clairvaux, Bernard traveled extensively, extending
the influence of the Roman Catholic Church and seeking to
win back to the fold those considered heretics. In so doing, he
gained wide recognition and was highly acclaimed as a mystic,
an intellectual, and an orator. His preaching, in fact, was
largely responsible for the Second Crusade (1147-49). In addition, as his fame increased, noblemen, bishops, princes, and
popes sought his counsel.

Bernard also gained recognition because of the many miracles that occurred in his ministry. It was reported, "From all
quarters sick persons were conveyed to him by the friends
who sought from him a cure."[1] The lame were healed, and
people were delivered from countless diseases and infirmities.
On one occasion, a boy, a deaf mute, was instantly able both
to hear and to speak as a result of Bernard's prayers. Shouting
and cheering arose from the crowd of onlookers who set the
boy on a wooden bench so that he could address them.[2]

The monk Gottfried tells of a young boy, who, having
been blind from birth, received his sight through the prayers
of Bernard. As his eyes opened, the boy shouted, "I see day, I
see everybody, I see people with hair." Clapping his hands in
delight, he exclaimed, "My God, now I will no more dash my
feet against the stones."[3]

## Hildegard of Bingen

Hildegard of Bingen (1098-1179) has been called "the most prominent woman in the Church of her day."[4] An important charismatic leader, she was the leader of a Benedictine convent near Bingen on the Rhine in what is now Germany. Widely recognized for her power in prayer, she was petitioned by many, including church officials, for her intercessions on their behalf.

Many came to Hildegard seeking healing, some from as far away as Sweden. She had no formula but seemed to rely on the inner leading of the Holy Spirit for the unique solution to each case. "Sometimes the medium used was a prayer, sometimes a simple word of command, sometimes water which, as in one case, healed paralysis of the tongue." Contemporaries reported that "scarcely a sick person came to her without being healed."[5]

Hildegard was also a visionary whose visions came while she was wide-awake and perfectly conscious. What she saw, she saw by "using the eyes and ears of the inner person according to the will of God."[6] In addition, she both spoke and sang in tongues. Her colleagues referred to these spiritual songs as "concerts in the Spirit."[7]

Because her experiences were not understood by some, critics denounced her as being demon possessed. She was defended, however, by her friend, Bernard of Clairvaux, who also commended her to Pope Eugenius III. In 1148, Eugenius personally visited her and, after investigating her revelations, "recognized the genuineness of her miracles and encouraged her to continue her course."[8]

## Dominic

Dominic (1170-1221), a contemporary of Francis of Assisi,

began a preaching order known as the *Dominicans.* They were distinguished for their missionary endeavors and their efforts in education. One of their chief goals was to win back to the Roman Catholic Church such groups as the Cathari and Waldensians by outstripping them in piety and zeal.

Many reports of visions and miracles surround the story of Dominic. On one occasion, when Napoleon, the son of Lord Cardinal Stephen, fell from his horse and instantly died, Dominic immediately went to the scene, stood before the lacerated corpse, raised his hands to heaven, and shouted, "Young man, Napoleon, in the name of our Lord Jesus Christ, I say to thee arise." Before the eyes of all those present, the young man arose and said, "Give me something to eat."[9]

On a journey through Europe, Dominic and his companions joined with a group of Germans, traveled with them for a time, and received their hospitality. Because Dominic did not understand their language, he could not talk to them. On their fourth day together, Dominic reproached himself for being so unconcerned with the eternal needs of his fellow travelers, and suggested to his companion that they "kneel down and pray God that He teach us their language for we are not able to announce them the Lord Jesus."[10] God answered their prayer, enabling them to speak to the Germans in their language. Astonished at Dominic's sudden ability to speak their language, the Germans listened intently over a four-day period as Dominic shared the Gospel.

### Francis of Assisi

Francis (1181-1226) was born the son of a prosperous merchant. As a young man, while praying in a church outside Assisi, he heard a voice say to him, "Go and repair My house which is fallen down." Interpreting "house" to mean the building in which he was praying, he immediately went to his father's warehouse, took a horse and a load of cloth, sold both and gave the money to the church for repairs. In retrospect, of course, Francis realized that "my house" actually referred to the Church generally.

Francis established the Franciscan order, a monastic order dedicated to studying the Scriptures, preaching the Gospel, praying, and helping the poor. Interpreting Matthew 10:7-19 literally, they elected to renounce all earthly possessions and to live in poverty. The order was endowed with great spiritual power and it has been called "perhaps the most thoroughly charismatic [order], in its primitive period, that the church has ever known."[11]

Indeed, Francis' preaching was accompanied by great power. Specifically, reports Butler, God gave Francis the gifts of prophecy and miracles.[12] Also, many healings occurred as a result of Francis' prayers. On one occasion, for example, while preaching in the city of Narni, Francis was taken to a man who was completely paralyzed. The man had expressed assurance that if Francis would come to him, he would be completely healed. When Francis entered the man's room, he made the sign of the cross over the man from his head to his feet. Immediately, the man arose fully recovered.[13]

According to Jacob de Voragine, a thirteenth century writer, Francis had originally been named *Giovanni* (i.e. *John*), but adopted the name *Francis* as the result of a miracle from God that had empowered him to speak French. De Voragine says, "Whenever he was filled with the fervour of the Holy Spirit, he burst forth ardently in the French tongue."[14]

## Vincent of Ferrier

During a time of illness, Vincent of Ferrier (1350-1419), a

Dominican preacher, received a vision of Christ who instructed him to "go through the world preaching Christ." When the vision subsided, he discovered that, indeed, he was completely well. Immediately, he set out preaching and teaching throughout Europe with astonishing results.

A fellow Dominican described Vincent as one whose words "struck terror in the hearts of sinners." In fact, such conviction accompanied his preaching that, at times, he was forced to curtail his sermons because of the overpowering sobs from the congregation. Everywhere he preached, countless conversions and remarkable miracles were reported. Butler reports that some *fainted*, or, as we would say today, *fell under the power*. During ministry in the Netherlands, so many miracles were wrought that an hour was set aside daily for the healing of the sick.[15]

Vincent is also reported to have possessed the gift of speaking in tongues. Butler says, "On the authority of reliable writers, various ethnic groups where he traveled and preached heard him speaking in their own language."[16]

### More Evidence

Many other examples could be given of the manifestation of the *charismata* among devout believers during this era. Jean of the Cross is said to have spoken in tongues often, once convincing two Moslems to believe on Christ by speaking in tongues in their native Arabic. St. Stephen (d. 1396), on his missions to Georgia, is said to have preached to the natives in their own language, a tongue he had never learned. St. Colette (1380-1447) is also said to have possessed the gift of tongues and to have spoken in both Latin and German.[17]

Best known, perhaps, is Francis Xavier (1506-1552). In his missions to the Far East, he is said to have spoken Japanese "as if he had lived in Japan all his life."[18] When the time came for his canonization by Urban VIII, much was made of the fact that Xavier possessed the gift of tongues and that he "spoke to the various tribes with ease in their languages."[19]

## Notes

[1] Augustus Neander, *General History of the Christian Church* vol. 4 (Boston: Crocker & Brewster, 1853), 154.

[2] Neander, vol. 4, 256.

[3] Neander, vol. 4, 256.

[4] Schaff. vol. 5, 371.

[5] Schaff, vol. 5, 372.

[6] Schaff, vol. 5, 372.

[7] Cutten, 41 and Schaff, vol. 5, 372.

[8] Schaff, vol. 5, 372.

[9] Francis C. Lehner, *Saint Dominic: Biographical Documents* (Washington D. C.: Thomist Press, 1964), 165-166.

[10] Cutten, 39.

[11] F. Sullivan, *Charism and Charismatic Renewal: A Biblical and Theological Study* (Dublin: Gill and Macmillan, 1982) 48.

[12] Thurston, Herbert and Donald Attwater ed., vol. 2 of *Butler's Lives of the Saints* (New York: P. J. Kennedy, 1963), 24.

[13] Placid Hermann, Ed., *St. Francis of Assisi* (Chicago: Herald Press, n.d.), 59-60 cited by John Wimber, *Power Evangelism* (San Francisco: Harper and Rowe, 1986), 166.

[14] Jacobus de Voragine, *The Golden Legend* vol. 2 (New York: Longmans, Green and Co., 1941), 597.

[15] *Butler's Lives of the Saints*, vol. 2, 32.

[16] *Butler's Lives of the Saints*, vol. 2, 33.

[17] Cutten, 40.

[18] Cutten, 45.

[19] Cutten, 44.

# CHAPTER 9

# The Cathari

IN CONTRAST TO THE MONASTICS who gave unequivocal support to the Roman Catholic Church, various groups and individuals emerged during the medieval period who were willing to leave the organized church in order to pursue what they considered a biblical faith and church pattern. These *come-outers* comprised many groups called by various names, but the most common designation for them was *Cathari*, meaning *pure*. This designation was a direct reference to their morally strict lifestyles, adopted in response to the Scriptures and in reaction to the political and moral corruption so prevalent in the institutional church. The designation was not new, but had, in fact, been used as early as the fourth century by the historian Eusebius in referring to the followers of Novatian.[1]

Knowledge of the Cathari and their beliefs is based almost solely on the testimony of their enemies. The only available documentation occurs in the records of heresy trials, and in tracts and instruction manuals for the treatment of heretics. Schaff rightly says, "Interesting as they are, they must be accepted with caution as the statements of enemies."[2]

The Cathari espoused various doctrines, but generally they held in common a tendency to be evangelical in faith and open to the miraculous ministry of the Holy Spirit. Directly related to this was a common concern over the lack of these elements in the established church together with its prevailing depravity and emphasis on ritual and form. According to Schaff,

> The exciting cause of this religious revolt is to be
> looked for in the worldliness and arrogance of the
> clergy, the formalism of the Church's ritual, and
> worldly ambitions of the papal policy. . . . The people
> wanted to get behind the clergy and ritual of sacra-
> ments to Christ himself.[3]

Their rejection of the value placed on externals by the institutional church expressed itself in various ways. For example,
they repudiated the idea that a church building was of any
religious value.

> God dwells not in houses made with hands. It is not the
> house of stone, but the good man and the good woman,
> and the community of such, that constitutes the Church.
> Prayer in the Church is no better than prayer in the closet.[4]

### The Consolamentum

In denouncing the highly developed form and ritual of the
Roman Church, the Cathari emphasized the inward and spiritual values of Christianity. They rejected all ordinances including baptism and the Lord's Supper. In place of water baptism, they taught a baptism in the Holy Spirit known as the *con-
solamentum*, received through the laying on of hands. According
to Augustus Neander, a nineteenth century Lutheran scholar,

> By virtue of this imposition of hands, whoever submit-
> ted to it in a suitable frame of mind, would be filled
> with gifts of the Holy Spirit, and purified from all sin;
> he would be made capable thereby for the first time of
> rightly understanding the deep things of Scripture. . . .
> This inward working of the divine Spirit stood to them
> in the place of sacraments.[5]

The Cathari experienced the supernatural ministry of the

Holy Spirit, including speaking in tongues. One woman is said to have spoken in a language unknown to her but recognized by others as Armenian.[6] Her enemies accused her of being under the spell of a wizard. Indeed, so widespread was the supernatural among the Cathari that the charge of witchcraft was a common justification given by the Roman Catholic Church for it attempts to destroy the movement.[7]

In reporting the miraculous phenomena that occurred among the Cathari, Neander supposed that they possessed a knowledge of the "hidden powers of nature."[8] However, he was seeking to explain these phenomena within the framework of his cessationist theology. The logical explanation is that the Cathari were personally acquainted with the Holy Spirit and His gifts. As such, they should be considered a genuine charismatic movement.

### Heretics or Heroes of the Faith?

Having found a source of authority, not only in the Scriptures, but also in a charismatic experience of the Spirit, the Cathari were looked upon as an affront to the authority of the institutional church. The Cathari thus became the objects of systematic attempts of annhilation by the Roman Catholic Church. Consequently, the Cathari were often burned at the stake or, at times, branded in the forehead with a hot iron marking them as heretics.

Many scholars consider the Cathari to be non-Christian, or, at very best, sub-Christian. This is based, however, on the biased, unfriendly testimony of their enemies. In contrast, John Foxe, the sixteenth century author of the famous classic, *Foxe's Book of Martyrs*, judged them to be true Christians and, in fact, forerunners of the Protestant Reformation.

It is obvious from the trial notes, especially, that the Cathari were well-versed in the Scriptures. Records show that they constantly and consistently appealed to Scripture to refute the charges of their accusers. In reaction to this, at the Synod of Toulouse in 1229, the Roman Catholic Church forbade laymen the use of vernacular translations of the Bible.

Schaff notes the highly exalted view of Christ held by the Cathari. Allegedly they denied the full reality of His human nature, saying that in the Incarnation, He passed through Mary like a pipe.[9] However, rather than an actual denial of Christ's humanity, it is more likely a reaction to the Roman Church's veneration of Mary as the *Mother of God*. There is, therefore, no reason to believe that they did not maintain a biblical, orthodox view of the person of Christ.

It is probably safe to say that the Cathari were devout believers who created an air of religious dissent that helped pave the way for the Protestant Reformation. Their dual emphasis on moral purity and the inner working of the Holy Spirit is characteristic of all renewal movements. Obviously, they experienced the charismatic gifts of the Holy Spirit and, therefore, deserve to be recognized as a genuine charismatic movement.

---

### Notes

[1] Eusebius, 280.

[2] Schaff, vol. 5, 462-63.

[3] Schaff, vol. 5, 463.

[4] Neander, vol. 4, 577.

[5] Neander, vol. 3, 595, 601; vol. 4, 575.

[6] Neander, 590.

[7] Clyde L. Manschreck, "The Occult Tradition in the Reformation," *Spiritual Frontiers* 6 & 7, nos. 1 & 4 (Autumn 1974 & Winter 1975): 104.

[8] Neander, 591.

[9] Schaff, vol. 5, 476.

# CHAPTER 10

# The Waldenses

THE WALDENSES BEGAN as a renewal movement within the Roman Catholic Church. Their vision was to see the Church renewed that it might truly reflect New Testament patterns. Rejected by the institution, however, they formed their own church which they claimed was a continuation of the early apostolic Church.[1] Like all renewal movements, they stressed the importance of the inner, spiritual life as opposed to the outward form and ritual of the institutional church.

Their distinctive platform included five main points. They urged the Church to return to the pure teaching of Scripture. They rejected the idea of purgatory and the infallibility of the Church. Christian laypersons were allowed to preach, and selling one's goods and giving to the poor were acts of consecration.[2]

### Peter Waldo

The Waldenses trace their origin to Peter Waldo, a wealthy merchant of Lyons, in southern France. Waldo lived in the latter half of the twelfth century and died in 1217. Around 1176, having obtained a translation of the New Testament, he read it and was especially struck by the words of Jesus to his disciples in Matthew 10:5-13 to go and preach without concern for material comfort. So impressed was Waldo that he gave up his possessions, keeping only enough to care for his family, and entered an itinerant preaching ministry reflecting what he saw in Scripture.

Waldo's life of devotion attracted others of like mind. Soon he found himself leading a sizable host of followers who shared his desire for the experiential reality which they saw in the Scriptures. Waldo organized his followers into bands, and two-by-two, they went out preaching the Gospel.

## Rejection and Persecution

In 1179, considering himself a loyal member of the Roman Catholic Church, Waldo applied to church authorities for permission for his group to preach. The Pope, Innocent III, refused his request, judging them to be, not heretics, but ignorant lay people. At this juncture, Waldo was forced to choose between obedience to God and man. Choosing to obey God, he continued the work already begun. Subsequently, in 1184, Pope Lucius III excommunicated the Waldenses.

## New Testament Christianity

The Waldenses searched the New Testament to find the biblical pattern for their lives and ministries. Consequently, they were open to and experienced the supernatural ministry of the Holy Spirit. *The New International Dictionary of the Christian Church* ascribes to the Waldenses "visions, prophecies, and spirit possession."[3] Like the Cathari, the Waldenses were accused of witchcraft because of these miraculous phenomena which also became grounds for persecution by the institutional church.[4]

## Divine Healing

Divine healing was a vital aspect of their belief system. The Waldensian confession of 1431 states,

Therefore concerning the anointing of the sick, we hold it as an article of faith, and profess sincerely from the heart that sick persons, when they ask it, may lawfully be anointed with anointing oil by one who joins them in praying that it may be efficacious to the healing of the body according to the design and end and effect mentioned by the apostles; and we profess that such an anointing performed according to the apostolic design and practice will be healing and profitable.[5]

## Equality in Ministry

The Waldenses recognized the responsibility of both men and women to preach, to baptize, and to administer the Lord's Supper. For them, the basis of ministry was the anointing or gifting of the Spirit rather than institutional appointment or ordination. Ministry was, therefore, open to all since it was the direct, free activity of the Holy Spirit which gave the right to bind and loose, to consecrate and bless.[6]

## Conclusion

Although the Waldenses were severely persecuted by the institutional church, they endured and in the sixteenth century, they identified with the Protestant Reformation. They maintained their separate identity, however, and may still be found in many parts of Italy. Although their stance on the *charismata* is not clear today, they were, in their beginnings, a charismatic movement.

## Notes

[1] See Alexis Muston, *A Complete History of the Waldenses and Their Colonies* (London: Blackie & Son, 1875); Schaff, vol. 5, 507.

[2] Lars Qualben, *A History of the Christian Church* (New York: Thomas Nelson, 1955), 182.

[3] J. D. Douglas, ed., *The New International Dictionary of the Christian Church* (Grand Rapids: Zondervan, 1974), 1026.

[4] Manschreck, "The Occult Tradition in the Reformation," 102-104.

[5] Gordon, 65.

[6] Schaff, vol. 5, 503-504.

## CHAPTER 11

# Martin Luther
# and the Reformation

W HEN MARTIN LUTHER (1483-1546) nailed his *Ninety-five Theses* to the door of the church in Wittenberg, Germany, on October 31, 1517, a major rift opened in Christendom. The action was a bold challenge to the authority of the Roman Catholic Church by one who was a priest and professor of theology. Luther strongly opposed the church's abuse of authority, particularly the selling of indulgences, a means by which the church, in exchange for money, completely forgave a person's sin without requiring repentance. Proceeds from indulgences funded the extravagance and pomp of the church hierarchy.

Luther had struggled long and hard over this issue and the larger issue of authority. He concluded that final authority resided with the Scriptures not the church hierarchy. Further, he concluded that salvation was by faith alone rather than by church appointed works and sacraments. This, of course, brought Luther into sharp conflict with church officials who insisted that final authority resided with the Catholic Church and that salvation was available only through the sacraments administered by those whom the church had ordained. This conflict culminated in a complete break between Luther and the Roman Catholic Church. It signaled the beginning of the Protestant Reformation.

## Luther and Miracles

Luther is sometimes thought to have been against the miraculous ministry of the Holy Spirit. This misconception has come about for at least two reasons. First, he wrote against the superstition and greed that had become associated with the miracles of the medieval Roman Catholic Church. Second, he opposed certain Anabaptists who claimed the direct leading of the Spirit for their bizarre teaching and actions.

Contrary to this, however, Luther has left clear evidence of his own belief in the personal and direct ministry of the Spirit. This evidence is presented in part by Professor Bengt Hoffman of Lutheran Theological Seminary in Gettysburg, Pennsylvania, in his book, *Luther and the Mystics.* He reports a conversation in which Cochelus asks Luther if he had received special revelations. Luther was silent for a moment, and then replied "'Est mihi revelatum,' yes, he had had revelations."[1] It seems that one of these was similar to Paul's experience of being caught up to the third heaven (2 Cor. 12).[2]

## Luther and Authority

Luther also claimed the direct activity of the Holy Spirit as a source for his own authority and teaching. In one of his early writings entitled *The Babylon Captivity of the Church,* he assures his readers that the truth he was presenting "I have learned under the Spirit's guidance."[3] In addition, when he was challenged concerning the source of his authority by church and civil officials at Worms, "he relied on the revelation of God to him—through the Word, but via the Spirit in a personal manner."[4]

## Luther and the Prophetic Gift

Many of Luther's early followers believed him to be a prophet. One of his first biographers, Johann Mathesius, mentions numerous prophecies spoken by Luther which were fulfilled. Mathesius then remarks, "With many sure prophecies he confirmed his doctrine."[5] Even his friend Melancthon, at one point, referred to Luther as *Elijah*, saying, "Thus the Holy Spirit prophesied of this third Elijah, Dr. Martin Luther."[6]

## Luther and Divine Healing

Luther prayed for the healing of the sick. Luther is quoted as saying, "Often has it happened, and still does, that devils have been driven out in the name of Christ; also by calling on His name and prayer, the sick have been healed."[7]

On one occasion, Luther's close friend and colleague, Philip Melancthon, became extremely ill and was at death's door. It is said that Luther prayed fervently using all the relevant promises he could repeat from Scripture. Then, taking Melancthon by the hand, he said, "Be of good courage, Philip, you shall not die." Melancthon immediately revived and soon regained his health. He later said, "I should have been a dead man had I not been recalled from death itself by the coming of Luther."[8]

On another occasion, Luther's colleague, Frederick Myconius, lay dying in the last stages of tuberculosis. When Luther heard about his friend's condition, he wrote him a letter that exudes faith for the miraculous. He said,

> I command thee in the Name of God to live because I still have need of thee in the work of reforming the Church. The Lord will never let me hear that thou art dead but permit thee to survive me. For this I am praying, this is my will, and may my will be done because I

79

seek only to glorify the Name of God.[9]

Myconius said that when he read the letter it seemed as though he heard Christ say, "Lazarus, come forth!" Luther's prayer was answered. Myconius was healed and outlived Luther by two months.

### Johannes Brenz

The emphasis on the miraculous ministry of the Holy Spirit was by no means limited to Luther. Johannes Brenz, another Lutheran reformer, was warned by an "inner voice" of the approach of the Spanish army at Stuttgart. The inner voice instructed him to go to the upper city, find an open door, enter it and hide under the roof. He obeyed, found the door, and hid as the voice had instructed. His hiding place was visited by a hen which daily laid two eggs for him until the danger was past.[10]

### Luther and Cessationism

In spite of his obvious belief in the immediate presence and power of the Holy Spirit, Luther and other Reformers of his day must share the blame for the wide-spread belief in a theory of the cessation of miracles. When challenged by Roman Catholic authorities to prove by miracles his own authority, Luther took refuge in the authority of Scripture and his own conscience. Miracles, he argued, were particularly suited to the apostolic age and were no longer necessary to vindicate the authority of the one who stands on the side of Scripture.[11] He drew on the same sort of argument in reaction to the Anabaptists who, in his opinion, maintained an undue reliance on the direct presence of the Holy Spirit.

His remarks were taken out of context and codified into a

legal system resulting in the Lutheran and Reformed wings of the Church harboring a distinct bias against the possibility of present day miracles. This bias reached its zenith, perhaps, with the publication of *Counterfeit Miracles* by Professor B. B. Warfield of Princeton in 1918. In this volume, Warfield declared that the Lord had not performed a single miracle on earth since the death of the original twelve apostles and those directly associated with them.[12]

## Welcome, Holy Spirit!

In spite of these unfortunate trends, the twentieth century has witnessed a new receptivity to the Holy Spirit among the spiritual children of Luther. In 1987, the International Lutheran Renewal Center coordinated an international, thirty-two member Lutheran Theological Consultation which produced *Welcome, Holy Spirit, A Study of Charismatic Renewal in the Church*. This study showed a marked receptivity to the charismatic dimension of the Spirit. Although it questioned certain traditional Pentecostal doctrines, it acknowledged that Pentecostals "have accurately perceived the Spirit's strategy" in that He is "calling believers to receive a personal outpouring of the Holy Spirit," and calling them to be "filled with the Holy Spirit in a way and to a degree that they have not done before."[13]

Luther would, no doubt, agree. The fourth stanza of his great hymn *A Mighty Fortress Is Our God* contains the phrase, "The Spirit and Gifts are ours." Souer's work in German, *A History of the Christian Church*, on page 406 of volume 3, describes Luther as "a prophet, evangelist, speaker in tongues and interpreter, in one person, endowed with all the gifts of the Holy Spirit."[14]

## Notes

[1] Bengt Hoffman, *Luther and the Mystics* (Minneapolis: Augsburg, 1976) 190.

[2] Hoffman, *Luther and the Mystics*, 154.

[3] Martin Luther, *The Babylon Captivity of the Church,* vol. 36 of *Luther's Works,* eds. Helmut T. Lehman and Jaroslav Pelikan (Philadelphia: Muhlenberg, 1958), 77.

[4] John S. Oyer, *Lutheran Reformers Against the Anabaptists* (The Hague: Martinus Nijhoff, 1964), 231.

[5] Johann Mathesius, *Luthers Leben in Predigten* (Prague: herausgegeben von G. Loesche, 1906), 399; Quoted by John Horsch, "The Faith of the Swiss Brethren, II." *Mennonite Quarterly Review* 5, no. 1 (1931): 16.

[6] John Horsch, "The Faith of the Swiss Brethren, II." 16.

[7] Gordon, 92.

[8] Gordon, 94.

[9] *Change the World School of Prayer* (Studio City: World Literature Crusade, 1976), C-35.

[10] Horsch, "The Faith of the Swiss Brethren, II." 15-16.

[11] Oyer, *Lutheran Reformers Against the Anabaptists*, 234.

[12] Benjamin B. Warfield, *Counterfeit Miracles,* (Carlisk, PA: Banner of Truth, 1983), 23-24.

[13] Larry Christenson, "Lutheran Charismatics," *Dictionary of Pentecostal and Charismatic Movements*, 565.

[14] This writer has been attempting to locate the original source of this quotation, a German work, through computerized inter-loan library services with access to over 2,000 libraries. The oldest reference to this quotation which I have found to date is in Stanley Frodsham, *With Signs Following* (Springfield: Gospel Publ., 1926), 329. The exact quotation and bibliographic data given by Frodsham has been repeated by Elmer C. Miller, *Pentecost Examined*, 19; Carl Brumback, *What Meaneth This?*, 92; and Morton Kelsey, *Tongue Speaking*, 51, who thinks it is "quite a plausible story."

# CHAPTER 12

# The Anabaptists

IF LUTHER WAS OPEN to the miraculous in his personal life, he regarded the supernatural with caution in his work of reforming the Church. Even though he broke with the Roman Catholic Church, he retained much of its liturgy and polity. He retained the rite of infant baptism, for example, as well as a state-supported, territorial church. The task of infusing the charismatic dimension into the normal worship of the congregation, therefore, fell to Luther's more radical contemporaries known as the *Anabaptists*.

### The So-Called *Radical* Reformers

Anabaptism began in Zurich, Switzerland, as part of the reform movement led by Ulrich Zwingli (1484-1531), a contemporary of Luther. A breach developed between Zwingli and two of his colleagues, Felix Manz and Conrad Grebel, when Zwingli decided to cooperate with the Zurich city council's decree that the Mass continue to be celebrated and that the destruction of images in the churches be halted.

This led to a complete break between Zwingli and his two colleagues who insisted on remaining true to the Scriptures in all reform efforts. For Grebel and Manz, remaining true to Scripture necessitated the immediate abolition of the Mass, the removal of all images from the churches, and the discontinuance of infant baptism. The Zurich council interpreted their stance as an affront to its authority and responded by ordering that anyone who did not have their children baptized within eight days of birth was to be banished from the region. Further, the council issued an order prohibiting the assembling of those who opposed the rite of infant baptism.

In response to the council's action, on January 21, 1525, Grebel and Manz, along with about twenty followers, met in Manz's home. After corporate prayer, George Blaurock asked Grebel to baptize him. Grebel consented and then asked to be baptized by Blaurock who proceeded to baptize, not only Grebel, but the entire assembly. According to Fritz Blanke, this marks "the birth of the Anabaptist movement."[1]

In Switzerland, indeed, throughout Europe, similar pockets of dissatisfaction arose regarding the work of the Reformers. Referring to Zwingli and Luther as *half-way men,* many felt that both were retaining too much of the old order. They said that Luther "tore down the old house, but built no new one in its place," and that Zwingli "threw down all infirmities as with thunder strokes, but erected nothing better in its place."[2] The *Radical Reformers,*[3] on the other hand, wanted to recover the apostolic order and discipline of the New Testament Church without compromising with the current order. C. Henry Smith says, "In fact, the whole movement was an attempt to reproduce as literally as possible the primitive apostolic Church in its original purity and simplicity."[4]

## Believer's Baptism

*Anabaptist* simply means *one who rebaptizes.* The Anabaptists insisted that baptism was for believers only and therefore excluded the idea of baptizing infants. For this stand, they were severely persecuted by both Catholics and other Protestants. In fact, laws were passed throughout most of Europe making adult baptism a capital offense. In spite of the severe persecution leveled against them, the Anabaptists increased in number and spread throughout Europe.

Because of intense persecution by both church and state, the Anabaptists often met secretly in homes, forests, or fields. There they read the Bible and prayed that the same Spirit and power that had been known by the primitive Church would come upon them. It was not unusual for the Anabaptists to dance, fall under the power, and speak in tongues.[5]

## Illumination of the Scriptures

The Anabaptists also believed that they experienced the illuminating presence of the Holy Spirit when they read the Bible. When Felix Manz was condemned to die as a heretic by the Zurich authorities on January 5, 1527, he was charged with "having boasted of special revelations." He was accused of pretending that "once or twice in prison and elsewhere certain epistles of Paul were revealed to him as if he had them before his eyes."[6] The court regarded this as proof that Manz had claimed individual revelation equal to Scripture. For this, he was drowned in the River Limmat the same day.

## The Prophethood of All Believers

In reaction to the ecclesiastical system of Roman Catholicism, the Anabaptists rejected an hierarchical structure of leadership and emphasized that ministry was the responsibility of the entire congregation. Thus, if Luther restored the idea of the "priesthood of all believers," then the Anabaptists restored the idea of the "prophethood of all believers." This concept is clearly seen in a Swiss Anabaptist document dated ca. 1532-34 and entitled *Answer of Some Who Are Called (Ana)Baptists Why They Do Not Attend the Churches.* In this document, the primary reason given for not attending the state churches is that those institutions did not allow the members of the congregation to exercise spiritual gifts according to "the Christian order as taught in the gospel or the word of God in 1 Cor. 14."[7] (1 Cor. 14 is the chapter that discusses the place of prophecy, tongues, and interpretation in the Christian assembly.) The author of the document chides Luther and Zwingli, accusing them of transgressing their own "original teaching" and of impeding "the rivers of living water" by not allowing the free exercise of Spiritual gifts in their congregations. He then says,

> It is Paul's intention that if one sitting by or listening receives a revelation or is moved to exercise his Spiritual gift or to prophesy, then the first shall hold his peace; and he Paul says that all may prophesy, one after the other.[8]

The author shows an obvious preference for a congregational-charismatic order for church meetings. Because the Holy Spirit resides in every member, and because, therefore, every member possesses one or more of His gifts for the edification of the whole Body, every member should have the opportunity to exercise that gift or gifts for the building up of the congregation. A Christian gathering dominated by one person cannot, therefore, be controlled by the Holy Spirit. He says,

> When someone comes to church and constantly hears only one person speaking, and all the listeners are silent, neither speaking nor prophesying, who can or will regard or confess the same to be a spiritual congregation, or confess according to I Cor. 14 that God is dwelling and operating in them through his Holy Spirit

with his gifts, impelling them one after another in the above mentioned order of speaking and prophesying.[9]

## Apocalyptic Extremists

Along with the rediscovery of prophecy and charismatic gifts many were also rediscovering the New Testament emphasis on the Second Advent of Christ. This was by no means limited to the Anabaptists, for even Luther believed that the end of the world was imminent and predicted that it would occur in 1532.[10] In fact, he rushed the publication of his translation of the book of Daniel, giving it priority over the other books of the Old Testament so that everyone might have the opportunity to read and comprehend the prophecy of Daniel before the end of the world.[11]

This expectation of the immediate end, when coupled with prophetic activity and intense persecution, tended to produce extremes in doctrine and excesses in practice. Not surprisingly, certain extremists emerged proclaiming apocalyptic visions of the impending end and of themselves as special end-time prophets. Dreams, visions, and prophetic utterances were the driving force behind their radical approach to reform which often included use of the sword.

On the basis of visions and prophecies, some of these extremists took the city of Munster by force and declared it to be the *New Jerusalem*. Their occupation was short-lived, however, for the Catholics quickly overpowered them, regaining control of the city. They wasted no time executing the leaders and slaughtering most of the people who had followed these leaders and their prophetic visions.

Because these extremists rejected infant baptism they were classified by both Catholics and Lutherans as Anabaptists. They were, in fact, totally different from the mainstream

Anabaptist movement which tended to be pacifist, rejecting all forms of war and conflict. Nonetheless, throughout history Anabaptists have often been vilified because of being mistakenly associated with the Munster fiasco. Only in the twentieth century has their true reputation been reclaimed from this erroneous association.

## Pilgram Marpeck

Before the Munster fiasco, Pilgram Marpeck, an Anabaptist leader in central Germany, had been warning his followers to beware of false prophets who claimed to be sent "to institute something different from that which Christ had instituted."[12] This is an obvious reference to the extremists who were even then claiming special authority and privilege through their many dreams, visions, and prophecies. Marpeck insisted that "the last days" had begun with the ministry of Christ and that charismatic gifts and ministries had continued among the faithful from then to the present time. A special commissioning of super-empowered, end-time prophets was therefore unnecessary.[13] Those who claimed such a commission were false prophets who had been beguiled by the devil and, in turn, deceived the unsuspecting and the naive.

Marpeck, however, makes clear to his readers that what he is writing is for the purpose of warning and not, "as some assume, as an argument to exclude divine miracles and signs." He continues, "Nor does Scripture assert this exclusion," for "God has a free hand even in these last days." He then mentions some who had been martyred for their faith and then miraculously raised from the dead. He says,

> Many of them have remained constant, enduring tortures inflicted by sword, rope, fire and water and suffering terrible, tyrannical, unheard-of deaths and martyr-

doms, all of which they could easily have avoided by recantation. Moreover one also marvels when he sees how the faithful God (who, after all, overflows with goodness) raises from the dead several such brothers and sisters of Christ after they were hanged, drowned or killed in other ways. Even today, they are found alive and we can hear their own testimony.[14]

Marpeck represents mainstream Anabaptists who affirmed the continuity in the true Church of "apostles, prophets, miracles, and teachers but all under Christ and in conformity to his gospel in Scripture."[15] In other words, revelation conveyed by genuine prophecy would not violate the revelation already disclosed in Scripture. It was not a matter of whether Scripture or Spirit had priority, but a conviction that the Spirit did not act in any manner contrary to Scripture.[16]

### Menno Simons

Menno Simons (1496-1561), a Catholic priest in Holland, joined the Anabaptists around 1535. In 1536, he began gathering scattered Anabaptists of northern Europe into congregations. Eventually recognizing Menno as their founder, these groups later became known as *Mennonites*.

In his *Treatise on Christian Baptism*, Simons is obviously not uncomfortable with the subject of speaking in tongues. He says,

Although Peter was previously informed by a heavenly vision that he might go to the Gentiles and teach them the gospel, still he refused to baptize the pious, noble and Godly centurion and his associates, so long as he did not see the Holy Spirit was descended upon them so that they spoke with tongues and glorified God. . . . Peter commanded that those only should be baptized who had received the Holy Ghost, who spoke with tongues and glorified God, which only pertains to the believing, and not to minor children.[17]

## The Anabaptist Legacy

The Anabaptist vision of the separation of the powers of the church and state became a foundational principle of modern Western society. Their rejection of force and coercion in matters of faith and their insistence on freedom of conscience have become hallmarks of freedom-loving people and nations throughout the world. George Williams, former Professor of Ecclesiastical History at Yale University, has said,

> The whole Western world, not only the direct descendants of the Continental Anabaptists, not alone even the larger Protestant community, but all who cherish Western institutions and freedoms, must acknowledge their indebtedness to the valor and the vision of the Anabaptists who glimpsed afresh the disparities between the church and the world, even when the latter construed itself as Christian.[18]

Direct descendants of the Anabaptists include the Amish, Hutterite, and Mennonite churches. In addition, their *free-church* concept influenced Puritan Separatists, Baptists, and Quakers. Even more important is their charismatic influence on succeeding generations. Mennonite scholar John H. Yoder has said that Pentecostalism "is in our century the closest parallel to what Anabaptism was in the sixteenth."[19] Anabaptism was certainly a charismatic movement.

---

### Notes
[1] Fritz Blanke, *Brothers in Christ* (Scottdale, PA: Herald, 1961), 20.

[2] Franklin H. Littell, *The Origins of Sectarian Protestantism* (New York: Beacon, 1964), 2.

[3] This name was coined by George H. Williams who authored *The Radical Reformation* (Philadelphia: Westminster, 1962).

[4] Franklin H. Littell, "The Anabaptist Concept of the Church," *The Anabaptist Vision*, ed. Guy F. Hershberger (Scottdale, PA: Herald, 1957), 121.

[5] Franklin H. Littell, *The Origins of Sectarian Protestantism* (New York: Beacon, 1964), 19.

[6] Horsch, "The Faith of the Swiss Brethren II," 15. See also George H. Williams, *The Radical Reformation* (Philadelphia: Westminster, 1962), 145.

[7] Paul Peachey and Shem Peachey, trans., "Answer of Some Who Are Called (Ana)Baptists. Why They Do Not Attend The Churches," *Mennonite Quarterly Review* 45, no. 1 (1971): 10.

[8] "Answer of Some Who Are Called (Ana)Baptists. Why They Do Not Attend The Churches," 11.

[9] "Answer of Some Who Are Called (Ana)Baptists. Why They Do Not Attend The Churches," 11.

[10] Johann Mathesius, *Luthers Leben in Predigten* (Prague: Herausgegeben von G. Loesche, 1906), 389; Quoted by John Horsch, "An Inquiry into the Truth of Accusations of Fanaticism and Crime Against the Early Swiss Brethren II," *Mennonite Quarterly Review* 8, no. 1 (1934): 83-84.

[11] John S. Oyer, *Lutheran Reformers Against the Anabaptists* (The Hague: Martinus Nijhoff, 1964), 238.

[12] William Klassen and Walter Klassen, ed. and trans. *The Writings of Pilgram Marpeck* (Scottdale: Herald, 1978), 96.

[13] Klassen and Klassen, *The Writings of Pilgram Marpeck*, 60-61.

[14] Klassen and Klassen, *The Writings of Pilgram Marpeck*, 50.

[15] Kenneth R. Davis, "Anabaptism as a Charismatic Movement," *Mennonite Quarterly Review* 53, no. 3 (1979): 225.

[16] John S. Oyer, *Lutheran Reformers Against the Anabaptists* (The Hague: Martinus Nijhoff, 1964), 86.

[17] J. C. Wenger, ed. Complete Writings of Menno Simons (Scottdale: Herald, 1965), 276.

[18] George H. Williams, *Spiritual and Anabaptist Writers,* vol. 25 of *The Library of Christian Classics* (London: SCM Press, 1957), 25.

[19] Davis, "Anabaptism as a Charismatic Movement," 221.

# CHAPTER 13

# The French Prophets

REFORMATION IDEAS BEGAN to make inroads into Catholic France after 1520. These ideas found fertile soil in spite of intense persecution, and Protestantism became a force to be reckoned with in that nation. After 1560, the French Protestants became known as *Huguenots,* and in 1598 they were granted freedom of religion by the Edict of Nantes.

When Louis XIV revoked this charter in 1685, severe persecution resumed. As many as 400,000 Huguenots fled to England, Prussia, Holland, South Africa, and the Carolinas in North America. Large numbers chose to remain, however, and of these, many were concentrated in the Cevennes Mountains of southern France. Because of the dynamic power of the Spirit in their midst, they became known as the *French Prophets.*

Their firm belief in the supernatural power of God arose from their diligent searching of the New Testament and prayer. They insisted, "God has no where in the Scriptures concluded Himself from dispensing again the extraordinary gifts of His Spirit unto Men."[1] Indeed, tongues, visions, prophetic utterances, and other supernatural phenomena were common in their midst.

## A Prophetic Anointing

One of the most outstanding phenomenon among these Protestant believers was the prophetic anointing that came upon small children. Children as young as three years old both prophesied and delivered discourses in perfect, fluent French even though this was not their native tongue. On one occasion, a fourteen month old child, who previously had never spoken, suddenly began exhorting "to the Works of Repentance" in a loud, childish voice.[2]

Adults were also seized by the Spirit and experienced the same sorts of spiritual phenomena. One woman, who had a reputation of being almost idiotic, under the power of the Holy Spirit, uttered discourses of such elevated character and in such good French that her hearers exclaimed, "This ass of Balaam has a mouth of gold."[3] One contemporary described a scene in which many "fell on their backs, they shut their eyes, they heaved with the breast, they remained a while in trances, and coming out of them with twitchings, they utter'd all that came into their mouths"[4]

## Speaking in Tongues

Speaking in tongues seems to have been common among the French Prophets. John Venett, who escaped to England, recalled hearing his mother speak French when under the power of the Holy Spirit. He was amazed, "because she never before attempted to speak a word in that language, nor has since to my knowledge, and I am certain she could not do it."[5]

Sir Richard Bulkey, a wealthy English nobleman, was converted through contact with French Prophets who were refugees in England. He tells of hearing one of their leaders, John Lacy, "repeat long sentences in Latin, and another refugee speak in Hebrew, neither one of whom could speak a single word in these languages when not in spiritual ecstasy."[6]

## Camisards

Hunted down by the marauding dragoons of the French government, these believers mounted an armed resistance. As a result of this resistance, they gained the name *Camisard* which means "night stalker." By 1711, the resistance was crushed and the movement dispersed. The faith of these French Prophets, however, could not be extinguished, and their spiritual experiences and exploits of faith were recounted throughout Europe.

John Wesley was acquainted with them and showed a cautious openness to those who had fled to England. When a certain Dr. Middleton contended that since apostolic times, not a single example could be found of anyone having exercised or having pretended to exercise the gift of tongues. Wesley replied, "Sir, your memory fails you again . . . It has been heard of more than once, no further off than the days of Dauphin,"[7] a reference to the French Prophets.

---

### Notes

[1] Michael P. Hamilton, *The Charismatic Movement* (Grand Rapids: Eerdmans, 1975), 75.

[2] John Lacy, *A Cry From the Desert* (London: n.p., 1708), 15.

[3] Morton Kelsey, *Tongue Speaking* (Garden City: Doubleday, 1964), 53.

[4] Hamilton, 75.

[5] Lacy, 14.

[6] George B. Cutten, *Speaking With Tongues: Historically and Psychologically Considered* (New Haven: Yale, 1927), 55.

[7] John Wesley, vol. 10 of *The Works of John Wesley*, 14 vols. (Grand Rapids: Zondervan, n.d.), 56.

# CHAPTER 14

# George Fox
# and the Quakers

A PEOPLE CALLED QUAKERS emerged in England about 1650. They preferred to be called *The Friends*, the popular name abbreviated from the group's official title *The Religious Society of Friends*. This, in turn, is derived from Jesus' words, "I have called you friends" (Jn. 15:15). Initially, they had referred to themselves as *Children of Light*, to their itinerant preachers as *First Publishers of Truth*, and to their movement as *Primitive Christianity Revived*.[1] Their adversaries, however, called them *Quakers*, a slur first pronounced by Justice Bennet in 1650 with the intention of ridiculing their peculiar response of trembling in the manifest presence of the Holy Spirit. Responding in 1678 to this name, Robert Barclay writes,

> And from this the name of *Quakers*, i.e. *Tremblers*, was first reproachfully crafted upon us; which though it be none of our choosing, yet in this respect we are not ashamed of it, but have reason to rejoice therefore, even that we are sensible of this power that hath oftentimes laid hold of our adversaries, and made them yield unto us, and join with us, and confess to the truth.[2]

## George Fox
Founder of the Quakers, George Fox (1624-91), was born in Leicestershire, England. From childhood, he expressed a

97

peculiar sobriety and yearning for spiritual truth and, as a young man, he went through a time of intense spiritual struggle to know God personally and experientially. Unable to find the help he needed from the priests of the state church and other religious leaders, he was at the point of total despair when he heard a voice say, "There is one, even Christ Jesus, that can speak to thy condition."[3] From that point, he began to experience the Spirit of the Lord leading and teaching him in a personal and dynamic fashion. In his search, he became particularly convinced of the priority of Christ within (Col. 1:27) and the Inner Light (Jn. 1:1-14).

## The Power Struggle
### Between Outward Symbols and Inner Light

The English church of Fox's day had broken with the Roman Catholic Church through the efforts of King Henry VIII. Since Henry's struggles with Rome had been political rather than doctrinal, the Church of England continued to be essentially the same as the Church of Rome. The main difference came with the Act of Supremacy, 1534, in which the English sovereign replaced the pope as supreme head of the Church of England.

Fox's emphasis on the reality and authority of Christ within the believer (Col. 1:27) and the Inner Light (Jn. 1:1-14) brought him into sharp conflict with the authority structure of the official church. Whereas the state church relied on outward ritual and ceremony to rule the people, Fox emphasized the responsibility of each individual to respond to the indwelling Christ of Scripture. He emphasized that the true Church consisted, not of buildings, but of God's true people. He preached against a professional, salaried ministry, declaring that authority to minister remained in Christ and expressed itself through all true believers. He proclaimed the equality of all people; therefore, he taught firmly against such practices as the use of human titles. This brought an outcry from the establishment of class-conscious England where, for example, the men of the lower classes were expected to doff their hats to the men and women of the upper classes and to address them by their social titles.

## Persecution

Because of the amalgamation of the church and state, Fox's views and practices precipitated open hostility from both ecclesiastical and civil authorities. Severe persecution erupted against the Quakers, and at one point about 15,000 were held in English prisons. Because of the squalid conditions, hundreds of these believers died while being held captive.

## Charismatic Phenomena

Charismatic phenomena were common amongst the early Quakers. Fox's *Journal* and *Book of Miracles* are filled with accounts of miraculous healings and other charismatic gifts. It is reported that on one occasion as Fox prayed,

> The Lord's power was so great that the house seemed to be shaken. When I had done some of the professors said it was now as in the days of the apostles, when the house was shaken where they were.[4]

In his *Journal*, Fox tells of the healing of fellow Quaker, John Banks, who had lost the use of his right arm and hand. The problem had begun with excruciating pain which descended from his shoulder into his arm and hand. In vain, Banks had sought help from physicians. Finally, with all hope gone, he had a dream in which he asked Fox to lay his hand on his shoulder and pray for healing. The dream was so real that he sought Fox and shared with him his dream. Fox laid his hand on him and simply said, "The Lord strengthen thee within and without." Banks stayed at the home of a friend that evening, and while eating supper, he suddenly realized that he had perfect use of his arm and hand. He was overwhelmed with gratitude and later said,

> My heart was broke into true tenderness before the Lord, and the next day I went home, with my hand and arm restored to its former use and strength, without any pain. And the next time that George Fox and I met he readily said, "John, thou mended, thou mended;" I answered, "Yes, very well, in a little time." "Well," said he, "give God the glory."[5]

One day, during his travels, Fox stopped at a Quaker home to spend the night. In the home, lying in a cradle, was a boy of about eleven years of age who had grown almost double and had never walked. Fox bid the boy be washed, dressed, and brought to him. He says,

> Then I was moved of the Lord God to lay my hand upon him and speak to him, and so bid the lass take him again and put on his clothes, and after we passed away.

Three years passed and Fox again stopped at this home. Met with an enthusiastic reception, he learned that, shortly after his departure, the parents had arrived home to find the boy well and playing in the street. In earnest, they begged Fox to stay "and have a meeting at our house for all the country is convinced by the great miracle that was done by thee upon my son."[6]

Fox also experienced the revelation gifts of the Holy Spirit such as discerning of Spirits, the word of knowledge and the word of wisdom. He often knew things supernaturally and says, "The Lord gave me a spirit of discerning, by which I many times saw the states and conditions of people, and could try their spirits."[7]

Speaking in tongues was also a common occurrence among the early Quakers. Edward Burroughs, a friend and colleague of Fox, speaks of Quaker meetings in which they waited together in silence before God for hours at a time. During these times of waiting they often experienced God's presence in a dynamic and apostolic fashion.

> We received often the pouring down of the Spirit upon us, and the gift of God's Holy eternal Spirit as in the days of old, and our hearts were made glad, and our tongues loosed, and our mouths opened, and we spake with new tongues, as the Lord gave us utterance, and as His Spirit led us, which was poured down upon us, on sons and daughters.[8]

## Conclusion

Undaunted by savage persecution, stonings, whippings, beatings, public hangings, and lengthy imprisonments, Quaker missionaries, in just one generation, let their light shine in various parts of the world from Turkey in the east to the English Colonies of the New World in the west. In one generation, the people called Quakers became the fastest growing movement in the Western world. By 1656, Fox had at least fifty-six associates who were traveling preachers, and by 1660, the movement could boast 40-60,000 adherents.[9]

This impressive sixteenth-century movement was, indeed, a charismatic movement. Their opposition to externals in religion and their emphasis on the interior life are characteristics of such a movement. Their own testimony confirms the importance which they attached to miraculous healings and other charismatic gifts.

---

## Notes

[1] Wm. C. Braithwaite, *The Beginnings of Quakerism* (London: n.p., 1912), 419; Henry J. Cadbury, *Quakerism and Early Christianity* (London: n.p., 1957); George Fox, *A Journal or Historical Account of the Life, Travels, Sufferings, and Christian Experiences in the Work of the ministry of that Ancient, Eminent, and Faithful Servant of Jesus Christ, George Fox*, vol. 1 of *The Works of George Fox*, 8 vols. (1706: reprint, new York: AMS Press, 1975), 105.

[2] Robert Barclay, *An Apology for the True Christian Divinity: Being an Explanation and Vindication of the Principles and Doctrines of the People Called Quakers* (1678; reprint, Philadelphia: Joseph James, 1789), 359.

[3] Rufus M. Jones, ed., *George Fox; An Autobiography* (Philadelphia: Ferris and Leach, 1919), 82.

[4] Jones, *George Fox*, 90.

[5] Henry J. Cadbury, ed., *George Fox's Book of Miracles* (London: Cambridge Press, 1948), 137.

[6] Cadbury, *Book of Miracles*, 125.

[7] Jones, *George Fox*, 185.

[8] George Fox, *The Great Mystery of the Great Whore Unfolded; And AntiChrist's Kingdom*, vol. 3 of *The Works of George Fox*, 8 vols. (New York: AMS Press, 1975), 13.

[9] See Wm. Sewell, *The History of the Rise, Increase, and Progress of the Christian People Called Quakers* (Philadelphia: Friends Book Store, 1774); Elton Trueblood, *A People Called Quakers* (New York: Harper and Row, 1966), 1.

# CHAPTER 15

# The Moravians

THE MORAVIAN CHURCH traces its beginnings to the pre-Lutheran Reformer, John Hus (1373-1415). Hus was a professor at the University of Prague and pastor of Bethlehem Chapel, the most influential church in Prague. One hundred years before Luther, he preached justification by faith and the supreme authority of Scripture. Because his preaching infuriated the church hierarchy, he was burned at the stake as a heretic in 1415.

In Moravia, his followers called themselves *United Brethren*. In spite of continuing persecution by the institutional church, they propagated their beliefs throughout their home province of Bohemia and into the neighboring province of Moravia. A new wave of persecution, the result of the Counter Reformation in the Catholic Church, forced hundreds of these believers from their homes. Between 1722 and 1727, many of these refugees found sanctuary at Berthelsdorf, Saxony, on the estate of Count Nicholas Ludwig von Zinzendorf (1700-60). There they established the community of *Herrnhut*, meaning "under the Lord's watch" or "on watch for the Lord."

## Count Zinzendorf

Count Zinzendorf (1700-60) was a committed Christian whom a contemporary described as "one of the most extraordinary personages that have appeared in the Church of Christ since the period of the Reformation."[1] Zinzendorf was reared by Pietist parents and was influenced by the leaders of the Pietist movement. Pietism, a spiritual renewal which had arisen within German Lutheranism in the late seventeenth century, was a reaction to the intellectual staleness that had arisen within Lutheranism one-hundred years after Luther.

## Fervent Prayer

Zinzendorf organized the Moravians into a church body with elders and pastors and encouraged them to seek God for a gracious outpouring of His Holy Spirit. Zinzendorf himself led the way with fervent supplications which sometimes lasted through the night. Community members soon began to gather of their own accord for prayer and at times would continue for an entire night. A spirit of prayer prevailed that touched the children as well as the adults. On one occasion, a group of young girls spent the hours of 10:00 p.m. to 1:00 a.m. "praying, singing and weeping."[2] The boys, at the same time, were engaged in prayer in another place.

## An Outpouring

During the summer of 1727, their prayers began to be answered in a remarkable fashion. On Sunday, August 10, about noon, while Pastor Rothe was leading the meeting at Herrnhut, he was overwhelmed by the presence of the Lord and fell to the floor. The entire congregation, overwhelmed by the Spirit and presence of the Lord, then sank to the floor with him. The service continued until midnight with prayer and singing, weeping and supplication.[3]

During a communion service three days later, God's presence was manifest in such a way that none of the participants could fully describe it. John Greenfield, Moravian historian and evangelist, says that they "hardly knew whether they belonged to heaven or earth."[4] Zinzendorf says,

> A sense of the nearness of Christ [was] bestowed in a single moment upon all the members that were present; and it was so unanimous that two members, at work twenty miles away, unaware that the meeting was being held, became at the same time deeply conscious of the same blessing.[5]

It was at this time that miraculous healings and other Spiritual gifts began to be manifest in their midst. Greenfield says, "Christian women and young people were filled with the Spirit and prophesied."[6] Zinzendorf says, "At this juncture supernatural gifts were manifested in the church and miraculous cures were wrought."[7] Zinzendorf also confirmed his belief in the supernatural ministry of the Holy Spirit with the following statement,

> To believe against hope is the root of the gift of miracles; and I owe this testimony to our beloved Church, that Apostolic powers are there manifested. We have had undeniable proofs thereof in the unequivocal discovery of things, persons and circumstances which could not humanly have been discovered, in the healing of maladies in themselves incurable, such as cancers, consumptions, when the patient was in the agonies of death, all by means of prayer, or of a single word.[8]

Although speaking in tongues is not mentioned *per se*, it did break out occasionally in the Moravian meetings. This is borne out by one John Roche who criticized the Moravians for reviving the practices of the Montanists. He also claimed that they "commonly broke into some disconnected Jargon, which they often passed upon the vulgar, 'as the exuberant and resistless Evacuations of the Spirit.'"[9]

On August 26, 1727, twenty-four Moravian men and the same number of women met and covenanted together to continue from one midnight to the next in continuous prayer. The twenty four hours of the night and day were divided among themselves by lot as each took their turn in keeping a continual fire burning on the altar (Lev. 6:13-14). Others soon joined this group of intercessors and the group grew to seventy-seven. The children also organized a similar plan.

The fervent intercessory prayers kindled a burning desire to make Christ's salvation known to the heathen. Missionaries were soon found throughout Europe, in North and South America, and in Asia and Africa. Moravian missionaries sailed to Georgia on the same boat as John Wesley and had a profound influence on his life. The German historian of Protestant Missions, Dr. Warneck, declared, "This small Church in twenty years called into being more Missions than the whole evangelical Church has done in two centuries."[10] The early Moravian Church was indeed a charismatic movement.

---

### Notes

[1] Edward Langton, *History of the Moravian Church* (London: George Allen & Unwin, 1956), 63.

[2] John Greenfield, *When the Spirit Came* (Minneapolis: Bethany, 1967), 25.

[3] Greenfield, 24.

[4] Greenfield, 11.

[5] Greenfield, 12.

[6] Greenfield, 60.

[7] Gordon, *Healing*, 67-68.

[8] Gordon, *Healing*, 67.

[9] Stanley M. Burgess, "Medieval and Modern Western Churches," *Initial Evidence*, ed. Gary B. McGee (Peabody: Hendrickson, 1991), 32.

[10] Greenfield, 15.

CHAPTER 16

# The Methodist Revival

### John Wesley

JOHN WESLEY (1703-1791) was born in Epworth, England,
the son of Samuel and Susannah Wesley. His father was the
rector of the Anglican parish in Epworth and his mother was
a brilliant woman who knew Hebrew, Greek, and Latin. She
diligently taught John and his six brothers and sisters academ-
ics and the ways of the Lord. John graduated from Oxford
with the highest degree of his day and was ordained to the
Anglican priesthood in 1728 at the age of twenty five.

While at Oxford, John and his brother, Charles, founded a
group whose participants became known as *Methodists* because of their methodical approach to seeking God. Every
evening from six to nine, they met for prayer and Bible study,
and every Wednesday and Friday they fasted. Once every
week they received Communion. This rigorous religious discipline did not, however, bring peace to Wesley's soul.

After a failed missionary journey to Georgia, he returned
to England where he continued his search. On the evening of
May 14, 1738, he found the inner assurance for which he had
sought so long. It came as he listened to a reading of Luther's
*Preface to Romans* at a meeting on Aldersgate Street in London.

> I felt my heart strangely warmed. I felt I did trust in
> Christ, Christ alone for my salvation and an assurance
> was given me that He had taken away my sin, even
> mine, and saved me from the law of sin and death.[1]

This experience profoundly affected Wesley's personal relationship with Christ as well as his public ministry. As he now proclaimed justification through faith in Christ alone, he was accepted by the masses but rejected by the church hierarchy. Wesley felt the sting of rejection, but he continued to seek God. In an all-night prayer meeting at this time, the Holy Spirit descended in mighty power on Wesley and his Methodist friends. He describes this event in his *Journal*.

> At about three in the morning, as we were continuing instant in prayer, the power of God came mightily upon us insomuch that many cried out for exceeding joy, and many fell to the ground . . . We broke out with one voice, "We praise thee O God, we acknowledge thee to be the Lord."[2]

As churches continued to reject him, he was forced to seek new avenues to minister. Encouraged by George Whitfield, he began traveling throughout England on horseback preaching in the open air. People gathered by the thousands, and multitudes were converted. The Spirit confirmed the Word with healings and deliverances, and with unusual manifestations such as falling, trembling, roaring, crying, and laughing.[3]

## Unusual Spiritual Phenomena

In his *Journal*, Wesley recorded many of the wondrous events.[4] In one meeting at Newgate, for example, as he began to preach, "immediately one, and another, and another sunk to the earth. They dropped on every side as if thunderstruck. All Newgate rang with the cries of those whom the word of God cut to the heart."[5] On another occasion, Wesley and his brother Charles took a walk in a meadow intending to sing psalms in praise to God. Just as they started to sing Charles burst into loud laughter. Before long, John too was laughing uncontrollably. "Nor could we possibly refrain, though we were ready to tear ouselves in pieces, but we were forced to go home without singing another line."[6]

Wesley himself experienced the miraculous benefits of the Gospel. He testifies to having been healed miraculously more than once. In one instance, he had been struck with such sickness that he could scarcely lift his head. This had been on Friday, and by Sunday, his condition had deteriorated.

> I was obliged to lie down most part of the day, being easy only in that posture. In the evening, beside the pain in my back and head, and the fever which still continued upon me, just as I began to pray I was seized with such a cough that I could hardly speak. At the same time came strongly to my mind, "These signs shall follow them that believe." I called on Jesus aloud to increase my faith and to confirm the word of His grace. While I was speaking, my pain vanished away, the fever left me, my bodily strength returned, and for many weeks I felt neither weakness or pain. Unto thee, O Lord, do I give thanks.[7]

On another occasion, he had been enroute to an important preaching engagement when his horse, Dan, had become lame. The resulting rough ride had given Wesley a pounding headache. As he lifted a silent prayer to God, he recalls, "Immediately my weariness and headache ceased and my horse's lameness in the same instant. Nor did he halt anymore that day or the next."[8]

### Charged with *Enthusiasm*

Wesley often found it necessary to defend himself against charges of being an *enthusiast*. This derogatory charge was directed at those who supposedly had forsaken reason and the

Scriptures in favor of subjective spiritual experience. A certain Mr. Church, for example, accused him of "inferring" that individuals under his ministry had experienced miraculous cures. Wesley replied,

> As it can be proved by abundance of witnesses that these cures were frequently (indeed almost always) the instantaneous consequences of prayer, your inference is just. I cannot, dare not affirm, that they were purely natural. I believe they were not. I believe many of them were wrought by the supernatural power of God.[9]

Also in this reply, Wesley expressed his belief in the continuance of miraculous gifts throughout the church age.

> I do not recollect any Scripture wherein we are taught that miracles were to be confined within the limits either of the apostolic age or the Cyprian age, or of any period of time, longer or shorter, even till the restitution of all things.[10]

### Speaking in Tongues

The supernatural was not limited to Wesley's open-air, evangelistic meetings. It was, in fact, an integral part of the lives of the early Methodists. In his *Journal*, Wesley includes a description of the revival at the Anglican parish of John Berridge in Everton. As the presence of God began to be sensibly felt, unusual phenomena began to occur with some crying out and some falling to the floor.

> This occasioned a mixture of various sounds; some shrieking, some roaring aloud. The most general was a loud breathing, like that of people half strangled and gasping for life. Great numbers wept without any noise; others fell down as dead; some sinking in silence; some with extreme noise and violent agitation.[11]

Speaking in tongues is not specifically mentioned in this account. However, researcher George B. Cutten ventures to say that speaking in tongues may have been part of this scene.[12] It is, indeed, possible that the groans, cries, loud breathing, and other inarticulate expressions so common among early Methodists may have included a form of speaking in tongues. This is especially borne out in an entry in Wesley's *Journal* dated July 30, 1739, in which he tells of a woman who "fell trembling to the ground. She then cried aloud, though not articulately, her words being swallowed up."[13] Even though this was not recognized as the biblical gift of speaking in tongues, there seems no logical reason not to consider it as such.

An early Methodist leader who did speak in tongues and who left a clear record of his experience was Thomas Walsh, a friend and colleague of Wesley. In the February 24, 1751, entry of his *Journal*, Walsh writes, "The influence of His Spirit wrought so powerfully upon me, that my joy was beyond expression." In his entry on March 8, 1751, he writes, "This morning the Lord gave me a language I knew not of, raising my soul to Him in a wonderful manner."[14]

Wesley himself never claimed the gift of tongues, but he defended the experience in his debate with Dr. Middleton. Middleton declared that the gift of tongues had not occurred since the first century and that any current claim to miracles without this gift was mere pretension. Wesley, quoting 1 Corinthians 12:11 which states that spiritual gifts are given as the Spirit wills, retorted,

> He who worketh as He will, may, with your good leave, give the gift of tongues where he gives no other; and may see abundant reasons to do so, whether you and I see them or not.

## A Second Work of Grace

Wesley's chief contribution to succeeding generations was his emphasis on an experience which Christians should seek subsequent to the new birth experience. He referred to this second experience as *Christian perfection* or *entire sanctification*. This was not *sinless perfection*. For Wesley this experience consisted of God's love so filling the heart that the power of sin would be broken and holiness of life would result. Wesley believed that a sanctified person could still make mistakes and even sin, but the mistakes would be related to the mind and making poor judgments rather than willful sins of the heart. The validating Scripture was Hebrews 12:14 which says, "Follow peace with all men and holiness [sanctification] without which no man shall see the Lord."

The idea of a work of grace subsequent to regeneration had not been emphasized since the fourth century and, along with the openness to personal, spiritual experiences, it became an important factor in setting the stage for the Pentecostal/Charismatic Movement of the twentieth century. For this reason Pentecostal historian, Vinson Synan, has referred to Wesley as the Father of the modern Pentecostal movement.[15]

## John Fletcher

Perhaps as deserving of this title as Wesley was his friend and colleague, John Fletcher (1729-1785), who became the systematic theologian of early Methodism. Fletcher, like Wesley, was an ordained priest in the Anglican Church. He spent most of his ministry as rector of the parish of Madeley where he made his home until his death. His most important work was *Checks to Antinomianism,* a defense of the Arminian theology of Wesley and a rebuttal of the Calvinistic branch of Methodism led by George Whitfield.

Fletcher's chief significance for Pentecostals and Charismatics is his penchant for *Pentecostal* language. He preferred *baptism in the Holy Spirit* to Wesley's *sanctification* and also seemed to see the distinction between *power* and *cleansing* in the two terms. In a letter to a friend, Fletcher exhorted him to hold fast what he had and be thankful for it until the Lord comes with more, "till He baptizes you with the Holy Ghost and with fire."[16] In a letter to Charles Wesley dated January 5, 1763, he says,

> What I want is the light and mighty power of the Spirit of God. As to my parish, we are just where we were: we look for our Pentecost, but we do not pray sufficiently to obtain it."[17]

Although at times Fletcher expresses lingering questions about the *charismata,* there is no doubt that he looked for a restoration of the power of the Holy Spirit such as transpired on the Day of Pentecost. This is borne out in a letter to Mr. Henry Brooke in 1784 in which he holds out a hope of a restoration that would restore to the Church "the spiritual glory which was bestowed upon her on the day of Pentecost."[18] Stevens has said of Fletcher,

> The dispensation of the Holy Ghost as the prerogative of the Church, he dwelt upon in the pulpit and in conversation continually. He lived and died in the assurance that this prevalence of the Spirit was limited in the world, only because the faith of the Church regarding it was feeble, and that the glorious wonder of a Pentecostal Church would yet be seen among men.[19]

Fletcher was widely read by nineteenth century holiness advocates who also incorporated his Pentecostal language into their teaching and writing. Wesleyan terminology was thus replaced by his Pentecostal terminology.[20] This helped set the stage for the twentieth century Pentecostal movement which emerged out of the nineteenth century Holiness movement. Early Methodism, a charismatic movement in its own right, thus became the womb that gave birth to the Pentecostal/Charismatic movement of the twentieth century.

---

### Notes

[1] Curnack, vol. 1 of *Journal*, 476.

[2] Curnack, vol. 2 of *Journal*, 122-125.

[3] See, for example, John Wesley, vol. 1 of *The Works of John Wesley*, 14 vols. (Grand Rapids: Zondervan, n.d.), 187, 189, 210, 271-73, 403.

[4] See also Steve Beard, *Thunderstruck: John Wesley and the Toronto Blessing* (Wilmore, KY: Thunderstruck Communications, 1996).

[5] Curnack, vol. 2 of *Journal*, 184-185.

[6] Wesley, vol. 1 of *Works*, 271-72.

[7] Wesley, vol. 8 of *Works*, 458-59.

[8] Curnack, vol. 3 of *Journal*, 236.

[9] Wesley, vol. 8 of *Works*, 457.

[10] Wesley, vol. 8 of *Works*, 465.

[11] Wesley, vol. 2 of *Works*, 483.

[12] Cutten, 70.

[13] Wesley, *Works*, 213

[14] William R. Davies, *Spirit Baptism and Spiritual Gifts in Early Methodism*, Jacksonville: Cross Fire Ministries, 1974), 12.

[15] Vinson Synan, *The Holiness-Pentecostal Movement in the United States*, (Grand Rapids: Eerdmans, 1971), 13.

[16] John Fletcher, vol. 2 of *The Works of the Rev. john Fletcher*, 2 vols. (London: Printed for Thomas Allman), 538.

[17] Fletcher, vol. 2, 513.

[18] Fletcher, vol. 2, 559.

[19] Abel Stevens, vol. 2, 271-272.5

[20] See Donald Dayton, "From Christian Perfection to the Baptism of the Holy Ghost," *Aspects of Pentecostal-Charismatic Origins*, ed. Vinson Synan (Plainfield: Logos, 1975), 39-54.

# CHAPTER 17

# The Great Awakening (1726-1750)

## Jonathan Edwards

COLONIAL AMERICA IN 1726 was in moral and spiritual decline. The challenges of frontier life and a series of brutal wars had demoralized many, and a shortage of churches and ministers had left many without spiritual care. Many existing churches had degenerated into formal religious institutions with no power to bring the much-needed change.

Jonathan Edwards, pastor of the Congregational Church in Northampton, Massachusetts, expressed his concern for the "general deadness throughout the land" and set himself to seek God for a "revival of religion."[1] Others also began to seek God diligently, and in 1726 a spiritual awakening broke out in various regions along the eastern seaboard. One of the communities where the Holy Spirit outpoured significant power was Northampton, Massachusetts. Indeed, an awesome sense of His divine presence permeated the entire community. Edwards reports that during the spring and summer, 1735, "the town seemed to be full of the presence of God." In every part of town, the Spirit of God was powerfully at work until "there was scarcely a single person in the town, old or young, left unconcerned about the great things of the eternal world."[2] Without any sort of planned evangelistic outreach "souls did as it were come by flocks to Jesus Christ."[3] Edward's church suddenly filled with those seeking salvation and with those experiencing the fruit of already being born again.

> Our public assemblies were then beautiful: the congregation was alive in God's service, everyone intent on the public worship, every hearer eager to drink in the words of the minister as they came from his mouth; the assembly were in general from time to time in tears while the word was preached; some weeping with sorrow and distress, others with joy and love, others with pity and concern for the souls of their neighbours.[4]

People from other communities often scoffed when they heard of the events in Northampton. Simply upon entering the community, however, their skepticism inevitably dissipated because of the overwhelming presence of God. As converts returned home, they carried the spirit of revival with them, and so the awakening spread.

During this time, Edwards preached his famous sermon, *Sinners in the Hands of an Angry God*. So powerfully did conviction of sin grip the people that Sunday morning, that the penitent cries for mercy drowned Edwards' voice. Hell became so real to the congregation that some clutched the backs of pews while others wrapped their arms around the pillars to keep, as it were, from being consumed by its eternal flames. Edwards made hell "real enough to be found in the atlas," writes Edwards' biographer, Ola Winslow.[5]

The power that accompanied Edward's preaching was not the result of his topic alone. Preaching on the terrors of hell did not monopolize his messages. He was, in fact, a very sensitive individual who could be melted to tears while contemplating the love and mercy of God. Neither was the power the fruit of oratorical skill, for Edward's normally read his sermons. His preaching derived its power from his prayer life.

He would spend whole days and weeks in prayer, and it was not unusual for him to spend eighteen hours in prayer prior to preaching a single sermon.[6] The result was a revival that not only transformed the moral and spiritual character of his own community but also that of the entire nation.

### George Whitfield

George Whitfield (1714-1770), a friend of the Wesleys, was a gifted preacher and a powerful communicator. Although he was an ordained Anglican clergyman, he was not denominationally prejudiced. In 1739, he arrived in America and traveled the length and breadth of the colonies on the eastern seaboard. Everywhere he went, shopkeepers closed their doors, farmers left their plows, and workers threw down their tools to hurry to the place where he was to preach. At a time when the population of Boston was estimated at 25,000, Whitfield preached to 30,000 on Boston Common.

Signs and wonders accompanied Whitfield's preaching. The power of God would move spontaneously throughout the congregations as he spoke. Following his message, further manifestations of the Spirit would occur. On one occasion, after preaching to a huge throng gathered outdoors, Whitfield surveyed the crowd and noted the amazing response.

> Look where I would, most were drowned in tears. Some were struck pale as death, others wringing their hands, others lying on the ground, others sinking into the arms of their friends, and most lifting up their eyes to heaven and crying out to God.[7]

Benjamin Franklin was a close friend of Whitfield. His testimony of the power of the revival is particularly significant since he did not profess to be a Christian. He recalls,

In 1739 there arrived among us from Ireland the Reverend Mr. Whitfield who made himself remarkable there as an itinerant preacher. He was at first permitted to preach in some of our churches but the clergy, taking a dislike to him, soon refused him their pulpits and he was obliged to preach in the fields. The multitudes of all sects and denominations that attended his sermons were enormous and it was a matter of speculation to me, who was one of the number, to observe the extraordinary influence of his oratory on his hearers. From being thoughtless or indifferent about religion, it seemed as if all the world were growing religious so that one could not walk through the town in an evening without hearing psalms sung in different families of every street.[8]

Many manifestations of the Great Awakening would be familiar to modern Pentecostals and Charismatics. Falling under the power, for example, was not unusual. Edwards refers to it as *fainting* and describes one meeting as being "full of nothing but outcries, faintings, and the like." Some were so affected "and their bodies so overcome, that they could not go home but were obliged to stay all night where they were."[9]

On one occasion, Edwards returned home to find the town "in very extraordinary circumstances, such as, in some respects, I never saw it in before." He remembers,

There were some instances of persons lying in a sort of trance, remaining perhaps for a whole twenty-four hours motionless, and with their senses locked up; but in the mean time under strong imaginations, as though they went to heaven and had there visions of glorious and delightful objects.[10]

Although he welcomed and defended outward demonstrations such as crying, groaning, and falling under the power, Edwards stopped short of accepting the validity of spiritual gifts such as prophecy, tongues, and miracles. As a staunch Calvinist, he believed that these "extraordinary gifts" had ceased with the apostolic Church. From that perspective, he tells of a man whom he believed was "deluded" into thinking that the revival was "the beginning of the glorious times of the Church spoken of in Scripture" and that "many in these times should be endued with the 'extraordinary gifts' of the Holy Ghost."[11] According to Edwards, the man was convinced of his delusion and lamented his error and the dishonor he had brought to God. Edwards then says, "The Spirit of God, not long after this time, appeared very sensibly withdrawing from all parts of the country."[12] Edwards interpreted this to mean that the Spirit was grieved with the "delusion" that had taken place. It is more likely, however, that the Spirit was grieved by this rejection of His presence and gifts.

This would seem to indicate that there were, at times, manifestations of the charismatic gifts. An opposer of the revival has left the following description of a local meeting. The reference to ecstatic utterances could include speaking in tongues.

> These meetings would continue till 10, 11, 12 o'clock at night; in the midst of them sometimes 10, 20, 30 and sometimes many more would scream and cry out, or send forth the most lamentable groans, whilst others made great manifestations of joy by clapping their hands, uttering ecstatic expressions, singing psalms and inviting and exhorting others.[13]

The revival had far-reaching implications. Reports in New England alone show 30-40,000 converts and 150 new churches. In addition, the revival changed the moral climate of colonial America and spawned extensive missionary work and other humanitarian enterprises. Colleges such as Princeton, Columbia, and Hampden-Sydney were established to equip ministers for the new congregations. The revival also contributed to the growing sense of political independence among the colonists. Harvard professor, William Perry, states, "The Declaration of Independence of 1776 was a result of the evangelical preaching of the evangelists of the Great Awakening."[14]

In conclusion, it should be stated that the Great Awakening had many characteristics of a charismatic revival. Although Edwards had strong reservations about the present validity of the *extraordinary* gifts of the Spirit, not all segments of the revival shared his reticence. Apart from this mitigating Calvinistic influence, the Great Awakening may be confidently embraced as a charismatic movement.

---

### Notes

[1] David S. Lovejoy, *Religious Enthusiasm and the Great Awakening* (Englewood Cliffs, NJ: Prentice Hall, 1969), 5.

[2] Jonathan Edwards, "A Narrative of Surprising Conversions," *Jonathan Edwards On Revival* (Carlisle, PA: Banner of Truth, 1984), 13.

[3] Edwards, "A Narrative of Surprising Conversions," 13.

[4] Edwards, "A Narrative of Surprising Conversions," 14.

[5] William Sweet, *Revivalism in America* (New York: Abingdon, 1944), 30.

[6] *Change the World School of Prayer* (Studio City, CA: World Literature Crusade, 1976), D-38.

[7] George Whitfield, *George Whitfield's Journals* (London: The Banner of Truth Trust, 1965), 425.

[8] Lovejoy, 35.

[9] Jonathan Edwards, "Revival of Religion in Northampton in 1740-1742," *Jonathan Edwards On Revival* (Carlisle, PA: Banner of Truth, 1984), 150.

[10] Edwards, "Revival of Religion in Northampton in 1740-1742," 154.

[11] Jonathan Edwards, "A Narrative of Surprising Conversions," *Jonathan Edwards On Revival* (Carlisle, PA: Banner of Truth, 1984), 71.

[12] Edwards, "A Narrative of Surprising Conversions," 71.

[13] Lovejoy, 77.

[14] Lawrence LaCour, Lecture on "Ministry of Evangelism" (Oral Roberts University, Fall 1989).

CHAPTER 18

# The Second Great Awakening (1800-1840)

As THE NINETEENTH CENTURY DAWNED, America was again morally bankrupt. A generation had come of age that knew little of the revival that had swept the nation sixty years earlier. Eight years of war had drained the nation's vitality leaving a dark cloud of spiritual indifference and moral degradation. Negative influences from the French Revolution were penetrating American society, and deism was at its peak of popularity. All of this resulted in a rise in profanity, drunkenness, gambling, and lewdness.

The General Assembly of the Presbyterian Church circulated a pastoral letter declaring they were "filled with concern and awful dread" at conditions which they beheld on every hand. They expressed the solemn conviction "that the eternal God has a controversy with this nation."[1] This concern prompted fervent prayer that precipitated a national spiritual awakening beginning on the east coast around 1800 and spreading to the western frontier.

### The Revival on the East Coast

Colleges on the east coast were hotbeds of rebellion at the time. Many students proudly professed to being atheists, agnostics, and skeptics, or *infidels,* as they were commonly called in those days. These same college campuses, however, became incubators of revival. At Yale, President Timothy Dwight, son-in-law of Jonathan Edwards, preached a series of chapel messages on infidelity. The spiritual stir resulted in one-third of the student body professing faith in Christ. Revival fires also engulfed Dartmouth, Williams, and other colleges and, from there, swept into the towns and cities.

## Revival in Kentucky

The revival on the east coast was tame compared to events across the Allegheny Mountains on the western frontier. There, James McGready, a Presbyterian pastor of three small congregations on the Gasper, Red, and Muddy Rivers in Logan County, Kentucky, sparked revival fires. In 1796, he led his congregation in signing a covenant to pray every Saturday and Sunday morning, and to devote the third Saturday of each month to prayer and fasting. Their focus was revival.

Four years passed with no obvious change, when suddenly a revival broke out that would eventually change the course of the nation. It started in a weekend meeting at McGready's Red River Church. The presence of the Spirit was so intense during the first two days of the meeting that the congregation was reduced to tears several times. On the final day, after the formal service had ended and the other ministers had left, two Methodist ministers, John and William McGhee lingered behind with the congregation. The Holy Spirit seemed to permeate the very atmosphere and weeping could be heard throughout the house. Finally, John McGhee rose to his feet to give one final exhortation.

> I exhorted them to let the Lord Omnipotent reign in their hearts and submit to Him and their souls should live. Many broke silence. The woman in the east end of the house shouted tremendously. I left the pulpit to go

to her. Several spoke to me, "You know these people Presbyterian are much for order, they will not bear the confusion, go back and be quiet." I turned to go back and was near falling, the power of God was strong upon me. I turned again, and losing sight of fear of man, I went through the house shouting and exhorting with all possible ecstasy and energy and the floor was soon covered by the slain.[2]

News of the event spread quickly, and McGready announced another meeting for the end of July at the Gasper River Church. Response was phenomenal. Some traveled a hundred miles to be in the meetings. Many came with tents prepared to camp out for four days. The church was much too small so they cleared away the underbrush from around the church, erected a preaching stand, and built simple log seats outdoors. This was probably the first planned camp-meeting in America and, for that matter, in the world.

The first service continued throughout the night. Sleep and physical comforts seemed to be forgotten as things eternal gripped the hearts and minds of the people. On Sunday evening, as John McGhee preached, the cries of the penitent almost drowned his voice. People throughout the congregation fell prostrate on the ground. Cries of distress over sin soon gave way to shouts of joy arising out of assurance of salvation.

### Barton Stone and the Cane Ridge Revival

Barton W. Stone, pastor of Presbyterian churches at Concord and Cane Ridge in Bourbon County, Kentucky, had attended the Red River meeting. Convinced it was a genuine work of God, he applied McGready's principles, and revival fires began to burn in his two congregations.

Beginning on August 6, 1801, Stone and several other ministers conducted a campmeeting at Cane Ridge that was exceptional both in terms of attendance and signs and wonders. One person counted 1,143 vehicles parked in the area, and estimates of those in attendance range from 10-25,000. James Crawford, one of the ministers present, reported about 3000 being slain in the Spirit.[3] Some broke out in loud laughter while others ran and shouted. Others even barked like dogs as they "treed the devil."[4]

The people, generally, accepted these manifestations as the work of God. They attracted the curious as well as unbelievers who often went away convinced of their divine origin. James Findlay, who was not a professing Christian, attended the Cane Ridge campmeeting and reported the following.

> The noise was like the roar of Niagara. The vast sea of human beings seemed to be agitated as if by a storm. Some of the people were singing, others praying, some crying for mercy in the most piteous accents, while others shouted vociferously. A strange supernatural power seemed to pervade the entire mass of mind there collected. . . . At one time I saw at least five hundred, swept down in a moment as if a battery of a thousand guns had been opened upon them, and then immediately followed shrieks and shouts that rent the very heavens. I fled for the woods . . . and wished I had stayed at home.[5]

The revival, perhaps because of the nature and number of manifestations, had its critics. On the other hand, Barton Stone and many others were convinced it was a genuine move of God. He said, "So low had religion sunk, and such carelessness had universally prevailed that I have thought that nothing common could have arrested and held the attention of the people."

Speaking in tongues was not necessarily emphasized; however, incidents of tongue speaking did occur in the various campmeetings throughout the country. The University of Georgia, for example, felt the effect of this revival, and when students visited nearby campgrounds, many were "seized" by the Spirit of God.

> They swooned away and lay for hours in the straw prepared for those "smitten of the Lord," or they started suddenly to flee away and fell prostrate as if shot by a sniper, or they took suddenly to jerking with apparently every muscle in their body until it seemed they would be torn to pieces or converted into marble, or they shouted and talked in unknown tongues.[6]

## Conclusion

Campmeetings, once introduced, immediately became popular. Presbyterians, Baptists, and Methodists often joined together in great general campmeetings with thousands attending. The revival grew, gaining momentum like a great tidal wave. Peter Cartwright, a Methodist preacher, stated, "The work went on and spread almost in every direction gathering additional force till our country seemed all coming to God."[7]

The Second Great Awakening was, in many respects, a charismatic revival bringing renewal to the churches and institutions of frontier America. The numerical results were as astounding as the spiritual manifestations. Between 1800-03 in Kentucky, alone, the Baptist churches added 10,000 new members and the Methodists, 40,000. Every denomination, in fact, experienced the fruit of the revival. The Spirit of God prevailed over infidelity and deism, and the religious character of the United States was assured for generations to come.[8]

## Notes

[1] William W. Sweet, *Religion of the American Frontier* (New York: Cooper Square, 1964), 55.

[2] Charles A. Johnson, *The Frontier Campmeeting* (Dallas: S.M.U., 1955), 35.

[3] Johnson, 65.

[4] Synan, *Holiness-Pentecostal Movement*, 24.

[5] Johnson, 64-65.

[6] Synan, *Holiness-Pentecostal Movement*, 24.

[7] Peter Cartwright, *An Autobiography*, ed. W. P. Strickland (New York: Hunt and Eaton, n.d.), 46.

[8] Frank G. Beardsley, *A History of American Revivals* (New York: American Tract Society, 1904), 100.

# CHAPTER 19

# Edward Irving
# and the
# Catholic Apostolic Church

EDWARD IRVING (1792-1834), native to Anna, Scotland, received an M.A. degree when he was sixteen, and in 1822, he was ordained with the national Church of Scotland. After working with Dr. Thomas Chalmers at St. John's in Glasgow, he took the pastorate of Caledonian Chapel in London. A powerful preacher, Irving soon attracted large crowds including members of parliament and other prominent citizens of London. A larger auditorium was built at Regent Square, but it also quickly filled to capacity.

### ". . . the gift of the Holy Spirit"
In 1827, Irving preached a series of sermons on baptism. In the course of his message, he referred to Acts 2:38.

> Repent and be baptized, everyone of you, in the name of Jesus Christ for the forgiveness of your sins; and you will receive the gift of the Holy Spirit.

He noted that, traditionally, this work of the Holy Spirit had been considered an inward gift of sanctification because the outward gift of power, according to some, had ceased with the passing of the apostles. He went on to say, however, that he could see no reason why the Church should not still receive the complete gift of the Holy Spirit including the gift of power. This, he said, had become obvious to him from the plain meaning of Scripture.[1]

Irving's view of the gifts of the Holy Spirit developed parallel with a doctrine of the incarnation that brought him into sharp conflict with church officials. It was his view that, although Christ never sinned, in the incarnation He had taken on the sinful flesh of humanity. For Irving, the power that gave Christ victory over sin and Satan was not inherent deity, but the indwelling presence of the Holy Spirit. Christ's earthly life was, therefore, a prototype of what every Christian may experience, at least in part. This empowering by the Spirit became, for Irving, a very important belief, and in commenting on the notion that spiritual gifts had ceased among believers, he said,

> If they ask for an explanation of the fact that these powers have ceased in the Church, I answer, that they have decayed just as faith and holiness have decayed; but that they have ceased is not a matter so clear. Til the time of the Reformation, this opinion was never mooted in the Church; and to this day the Roman Catholics, and every other portion of the Church but ourselves, maintain the very contrary.[2]

### A Charismatic Outbreak in Scotland

While Irving was grappling with these issues, a charismatic revival was breaking out in the Gareloch and Port Glasgow regions of western Scotland. In the town of Fernicarry, a young lady named Mary Campbell lay dying of tuberculosis. On March 28, 1830, while praying with her sister and a friend, the Holy Spirit came upon her with mighty power

and constrained her to speak at great length, and with

superhuman strength, in an unknown tongue, to the great astonishment of all who heard, and to her own great edification and enjoyment in God."[3]

Meanwhile, in the Port Glasgow area, prayer meetings were being held in which participants were praying for a restoration of spiritual gifts to the Church. In April 1830, James MacDonald had a spiritual experience which he identified as the baptism in the Holy Spirit. A few moments after this experience, he went to the room of his sister, Margaret, who was near death, and commanded her to arise from her bed. She arose miraculously healed.

James then felt prompted to write a letter to Mary Campbell with whom he and his family were acquainted. He told her of Margaret's healing, and he commanded her to arise and be healed as well. When Mary Campbell read the letter, she too was healed. She writes,

> a power which no words can describe; it was felt to be indeed the voice of Christ . . . I was verily made in a moment to stand upon my feet, leap and walk, sing and rejoice."[4]

A few evenings later on April 18, 1830, both George and James spoke in tongues for the first time. The next night, they not only spoke in tongues but also interpreted tongues. The first interpretation was "Behold! He cometh—Jesus cometh!" These events stirred the whole area, and by the middle of May, the MacDonald house was filled every day with people from all parts of England, Scotland, and Ireland.

Irving received the reports of these events with a mix of excitement and caution. "I felt it to be a matter of too great concern to yield up my faith to anything but the clearest evidence."[5] He realized that if true, "it would revolutionize the

Church and make such an upturning as the world had not seen."[6] After discussing the events with eyewitnesses, including members of his own church, and interviewing the Spirit-baptized ones themselves, Irving concluded that this, indeed, was a genuine work of the Holy Spirit.

## Events in London

Irving began to testify publicly of the events to his congregation, and he encouraged prayer meetings for the purpose of seeking spiritual gifts. As a result, almost a year later on April 31, 1831, Mrs. Cardale, the wife of a prominent London lawyer and a member of Irving's church, spoke in tongues at a home prayer meeting. Six months later, on October 30, Miss Hall spoke in tongues in the vestry of Regent Square Church. The following Sunday, several believers brought forth utterances in tongues and prophecy during the morning worship service. Needless to say, this caused no small stir.[7]

Although the majority of the congregation supported Irving in his quest for spiritual gifts, several key leaders vehemently opposed him. For three months, similar manifestations of the Spirit occurred. At that point, however, the trustees of the Regent Square Church appealed to the presbytery of the denomination to intervene. In a church trial, Irving was found guilty of allowing individuals to lead public worship who had no official appointment or ordination. He was removed from the pastorate of Regent Square Church, and on May 4, he was locked out of his church.

The presbytery then proceeded to try Irving on charges of holding heretical views concerning the person and humanity of Christ.[8] Subsequently, on March 13, 1833, he was found guilty of the charges and was excommunicated from the ministry of the Church of Scotland. A majority of Regent Square members left with Irving and formed a new congregation on Newman Street called the *Catholic Apostolic Church*.

Irving and his associates believed that God was restoring all the gifts, ministries, and power of the early Church. During the next two years, twelve men in the congregation were set apart as *apostles*. This was done primarily on the basis of prophetic utterance. Irving himself was appointed as *angel* or *pastor* of the congregation and throughout Great Britain, other like-minded churches and pastors began linking themselves with the Newman Street Church.[9]

## The Standing Sign

At this time, Irving began unreservedly to formulate his thoughts on the baptism in the Holy Spirit and spiritual gifts. His extensive writings on the subject reveal his view of Spirit baptism as an endowment of power subsequent to regeneration. He also speaks of Spirit baptism "whose standing sign, if we err not, is the speaking with tongues."[10] Thus, seventy years before the modern Pentecostal revival began, Irving had already formulated the classic Pentecostal doctrine.

Irving also understood the devotional aspect of speaking in tongues. He says,

> Therefore it is nothing to be doubted that tongues are a great instrument for personal edification, however mysterious it may seem to us; and they are on that account greatly to be desired.

Irving saw that the outcome for those who would practice this private, devotional tongues would be "that they may prophesy and edify the Church when they themselves have been edified."[11]

Irving's involvement with the Catholic Apostolic Church proved to be short-lived. In September, 1834, already weakened in health, he traveled by horseback from London to Glasgow where he founded a new congregation. When his health deteriorated rapidly, however, he was diagnosed with consumption. Finally confined to bed, he died on December 7, 1834, at the age of 42. His funeral service, conducted at the Glasgow Cathedral, was attended by a large crowd, among whom were many who had opposed him. The sermon text was 2 Samuel 3:38, "Know ye not that there is a prince and a great man fallen this day in Israel."

George Strachan, a student of Irving's life and theology, states that Irving's writings during his last years reveal a "lucid and ordered mind, unfolding a complete theological system."[12] Larry Christenson, a Lutheran charismatic, notes,

> He was a man ahead of his time, pointing to things yet future for the great body of the Church. He was a forerunner not only of the Catholic Apostolic Church in a direct sense, but of the entire pentecostal phenomenon of the twentieth century. The things he said and did, his emphases and concerns, largely rejected in his own day, have become common place in the Pentecostal Movement of our time.[13]

The question arises concerning whether Irving himself ever spoke in tongues. Because he never claimed to have experienced Spirit baptism or to have spoken in tongues, many have concluded that he did not. Others, however, believe otherwise. David Dorries, for example, who wrote a doctoral dissertation defending Irving's christology, believes that he did. He notes Irving's extensive and intimate writings about the purpose and function of Spirit baptism during the final years of his life. He asks, "Would Irving have so untiringly committed himself to leading others into the deeper reaches of this dimension of power had he himself been a castaway?"[14] In addition, a work published in 1883 quotes Horace Bushnell as saying,

> Mr. Irving was not only gifted with the power of heal-ing the sick, but he was overtaken unexpectedly with the strange gift of tongues: vis., an ecstatic utterance, in words and sounds, which neither he nor any that heard him understood.[15]

## Conclusion

The leaders of the Catholic Apostolic Church appointed no successors, perhaps because they believed in the imminent Second Advent of Christ. In 1901, the last apostle of the church died signaling, for all practical purposes, the end of the Catholic Apostolic Church. That same year, half way around the world in Topeka, Kansas, a small group of Bible school students experienced an outpouring of the Holy Spirit and spoke in tongues. Although they seem to have had no direct connection with the Catholic Apostolic Church, they too had identified speaking in tongues as the evidence of Spirit bap-tism. The modern Pentecostal/Charismatic revival that would sweep the earth in the twentieth century was now beginning. For Irving, this was familiar ground. He had arrived there seventy years earlier.

---

### Notes

[1] C. Gordon Strachan, *The Pentecostal Theology of Edward Irving* (London: Darton, Longmann & Todd, 1973), 55.

[2] Strachan, 82.

[3] Edward Irving, "Facts Connected With Recent Manifestations of Spiritual Gifts," *Frasers Magazine*, Jan. 1832, cited by Strachan, 66.

[4] Robert Norton M.D., *Memoirs of James and George MacDonald of Port Glasgow* (n.p.: n.d.), 109-110, cited by Strachan 68.

[5] Strachan, 69.

[6] Strachan, 69.

[7] Strachan, 13.

[8] For a thorough defense of Irving and his orthodoxy see David W. Dorries, "Nineteenth Century British Christological Controversy, Centering Upon Edward Irving's Doctrine of Christ's Human Nature," (Ph.D. Thesis, University of Aberdeen, Scotland, 1988).

[9] David Dorries, "Edward Irving and the Standing Sign," *Initial Evidence*, ed. Gary B. McGee (Peabody, MA: Hendrickson, 1991), 46.

[10] Dorries, "Edward Irving and the Standing Sign," 49.

[11] Dorries, 36.

[12] Strachan, 21.

[13] Larry Christenson, "Pentecostalism's Forgotten Forerunner," *Aspects of Pentecostal/Charismatic Origins* (Plainfield, NJ: Logos, 1975), 20.

[14] Dorries, 53.

[15] Sir Thomas Erskine, *The Supernatural Gifts of the Spirit*, ed. R. Kelso Carter (Philadelphia: Words of Faith, 1883), 13.

# CHAPTER 20

# The 19th Century Forerunners of the Modern Pentecostal/Charismatic Movement

THE HOLINESS MOVEMENT of the nineteenth century began as a renewal movement within the Methodist Church. It was an attempt to recover both the religious fervor of the previous century and John Wesley's teaching of a second work of grace in the life of the believer. In addition, a concerted effort was extended to recovering the faith of the primitive Church, and this, in particular, opened the door for the miraculous gifts of the Spirit to be manifest.

Beginning in the Methodist Church, this renewal movement eventually exerted an influence on almost every denomination in America. Non-Wesleyans usually preferred non-Wesleyan terminology to describe their quest for a higher level of Christian experience. Presbyterians, for example, often referred to it as the *higher Christian life*. Baptists spoke of it as the *rest of faith*. Eventually, almost all adopted Pentecostal terminology and referred to it as the *baptism in the Holy Spirit*.

## Phoebe Palmer

The most prominent and influential leader in this nineteenth century quest for a higher plane of Christian experience was Phoebe Worrall Palmer (1807-1874). Palmer, wife of prominent New York physician Dr. Walter Palmer (1804-74), was a Methodist lay person. She was never ordained, yet so profound was her influence that she has been called "the most influential female theologian the church has yet produced."[1]

In 1840, Palmer became the leader of the Tuesday Meeting for the Promotion of Holiness. This meeting, conducted in the Palmer's spacious parlor, was attended by at least four Methodist bishops as well as by many other prominent churchmen both within and without the Methodist tradition. Palmer also became a prolific writer, authoring three books, including: *The Way of Holiness* (1843), *The Promise of the Father* (1859), *Four Years in the Old World* (1865). In addition, from 1864-74, she edited and published *The Guide to Holiness*, the most influential Holiness periodical of that era.

With Walter's full support, Phoebe also traveled extensively, ministering throughout the United States, Canada, and Great Britain. In the latter part of her ministry Walter traveled with her and assisted in the meetings. Descriptions of their meetings rival those of Wesley, Finney, and Moody. Hundreds and even thousands would be converted during protracted meetings that ran anywhere from a few days to several weeks. Hundreds more would claim to have received the second blessing of sanctification or the baptism in the Holy Spirit, as it was also called.

In the city of Newcastle, England, for example, Phoebe says that "the Lord was saving the people by scores daily."[2] At the time of her writing, over two thousand names of people who had received the blessing "of pardon or purity" had been recorded. Such an impact was being made that "now the entire community seems ready to acknowledge its [the revival's] power."[3]

These revivals were attended by great spiritual power which was, perhaps, the key to their success. Writing from Sunderland she says that there is such a sense of the divine presence that "people are weeping all over the house."[4] In Newcastle she states that "the power of God is sensibly felt to be present to heal."[5] She also speaks of those who "felt the girdings of almighty power in an unusual manner" and of the "tokens of divine presence" in our midst.[6] For Palmer, this sort of experiential revivalism represented "a resuscitation of primitive Christianity and primitive Methodism."[7]

Speaking in tongues probably occurred at times in her meetings. Writing from England, she says that the emphasis of the afternoon meetings is "the full baptism of the Holy Spirit, as received by the one hundred and twenty disciples on the day of Pentecost."[8] For Palmer, then, Spirit baptism affected one's speech even as the speech of the one-hundred and twenty had been affected on the Day of Pentecost. In describing one meeting, she says that "the baptism of fire descended; and, as in the early days of Christianity, utterance as a restraining gift was also given."[9] On another occasion, a local preacher came forward and was the first to receive "the tongue of fire." According to Palmer, he then "spake as the Spirit gave utterance."[10]

Through Palmer's extensive influence, Pentecostal language finally replaced Wesleyan terminology in describing the second blessing. Instead of *sanctification*, it was now *the baptism of the Holy Ghost*, and instead of *cleansing from sin*, the blessing now consisted of an *endowment of power*. These trends were important developments as the Church moved toward the twentieth century and the explosion of the modern Pentecostal/Charismatic movement.

## Charles Finney

Charles Grandson Finney (1792-1873) was converted at the age of twenty-nine and became one of the most successful evangelists of modern times. A lawyer at the time of his conversion, Finney first aligned himself with the Presbyterian Church, but later he joined the Congregational Church. He was known for his revivalistic innovations such as the altar call and *anxious seat* and for his powerful, logical preaching. Thousands were converted and entire communities were transformed through his ministry. His *Autobiography* and *Lectures on Revival* are still perused by students of revival.

At the time of his conversion, Finney had an experience which he later identified as the baptism in the Holy Spirit. He recalled that he "wept aloud with joy and love" and "literally bellowed out the unutterable gushings of my soul," a possible reference to speaking in tongues.[11]

Although Finney did not practice praying for the sick, there were scattered reports of miraculous healings through his ministry. In addition, at least two mentally ill persons were healed in his meetings. On one occasion, he was informed that a certain woman who was unconverted was ill and would not live through the night. After a time of intense prayer for the woman, he experienced a settled peace in his mind and upon meeting her husband the next day, he made a bold declaration. He said, "Brother W____, she will not die with this sickness; you may rely upon it. And she will never die in her sins."[12] The woman recovered and shortly thereafter was converted to Christ.

Remarkable manifestations of the Spirit accompanied Finney's meetings. Falling under the power, weeping, and crying out were not uncommon occurrences. While praying at the close of a meeting in Rome, New York, he could hear the "sobs and sighs" of the people throughout the house. He quickly closed the prayer and rose suddenly from his knees.

At this very moment a young man by the name of W____, a clerk in Mr. H____'s store, being one of the first young men in the place, so nearly fainted, that he fell upon some young men who stood near him; and they all of them partially swooned away, and fell together.[13]

The power of Finney's revivals often impacted entire communities. A student in Rochester Academy, Charles P. Bush, later to become a leading pastor in New York City, was converted under Finney's ministry in Rochester, New York. He gives this account of that first revival in his native city.

The whole community was stirred. Religion was the topic of conversation, in the house, in the shop, in the office and on the street. The only theater in the city was converted into a livery stable; the only circus into a soap and candle factory. Grog shops were closed; the Sabbath was honored; the sanctuaries were thronged with happy worshippers; a new impulse was given to every philanthropic enterprise; the fountains of benevolence were opened, and men lived to good.[14]

In 1835, Finney became the professor of Systematic Theology at the newly formed Oberlin College in Oberlin, Ohio. It was here that he and Asa Mahan, the first president of Oberlin, forged what became known as *Oberlin Theology*. *Oberlin Theology* referred to *the second blessing* as *the baptism in the Holy Spirit*. They identified this experience as an empowerment for effective Christian service rather than as cleansing from original sin. In commenting on the lack in a certain pastor's life and ministry, Finney observed,

He had fallen short of receiving the baptism of the

Holy Ghost which is indispensable to ministerial success. When Christ commissioned his apostles to go and preach, he told them to abide at Jerusalem till they were endued with power from on high. This power, as everyone knows, was the baptism of the Holy Ghost poured out upon them on the day of Pentecost. This was an indispensable qualification for success in ministry.[15]

Finney's revival techniques of protracted meetings and public professions of faith were adopted throughout the Holiness movement and carried over into the Pentecostal movement. These techniques, along with his theory of a subsequent empowerment of the Spirit, played a major role in preparing the way for the Pentecostal/Charismatic revival of the twentieth century.

## A. J. Gordon

A. J. Gordon (1836-1895), founder of Gordon College, was the pastor of Clarendon Street Baptist Church in Boston, Massachusetts, for twenty-five years. A voluminous writer, he authored such works as *The Ministry of Healing, The Two-Fold Life* and *The Ministry of The Holy Spirit*.[16] One writer has described him as "a major figure on the way to Pentecostalism."[17]

In *The Ministry of The Holy Spirit,* Gordon clearly delineates a charismatic theology by identifying the baptism in the Holy Spirit as an endowment of power subsequent to conversion. In his discussion of Spirit baptism, he also mentions the manifestation of tongues at Pentecost (Acts 2:4) and the manifestation of tongues and prophecy when Paul laid his hands on the new Ephesian believers (Acts 19:1-7). The Ephesians, Gordon says, "exhibited the traits of the Spirit common to the other disciples of the apostolic age . . . and whatsoever relations believers held to the Spirit in the beginning, they have a right to claim today."[18]

In his work, *The Two-Fold Life,* Gordon declares, "It is still our privilege to pray for the baptism of the Spirit, and to tarry in supplication until we be endued with power from on high."[19] In *The Ministry of Healing* he not only defends divine healing as a ministry of the Church but also says that even the gifts of tongues and prophecy "do not seem to be confined within the first age of the Church."[20]

Further proof of Gordon's charismatic tendencies is the fact that he was profoundly influenced by the writings of Edward Irving. This is borne out in *The Ministry of Healing* where he devotes six pages to Irving and speaks of him in glowing terms. He refers to Irving as "a man of wonderful endowments" and says that "he was accused of offering strange fire upon the altar of his church because he thought to relight the fire of Pentecost."[21]

Gordon's writings were widely read in the latter part of the nineteenth century and influenced many toward an openness to miraculous manifestations. Some of his terminology such as *the sealing of the Holy Spirit* may have been adopted by early Pentecostals who use the same expression in their own writings.[22]

A more direct influence was through Elizabeth Baker who attended his church before founding Elim Tabernacle and Rochester Bible Training Center in Rochester, New York. Elim Tabernacle and Rochester Bible Training Center became an important center for Pentecostalism during the early days of the movement. Pentecostal historian, Carl Brumback, describes the school as "the first permanent school to make a genuine impression on the Movement."[23]

Gordon's theology would place him in the midst of the modern Charismatic Movement if he were alive today. His belief in a subsequent empowering of the Spirit coupled with a persuasion that charismatic gifts, including speaking in tongues, are yet valid and desirable, is clearly the essence of modern charismatic theology. Gordon's theological stance clearly identifies him as a *charismatic* Christian.

## Dwight L. Moody

D. L. Moody (1837-1899), the most prominent evangelist during the latter half of the nineteenth century, also embraced the teaching of a baptism in the Holy Spirit subsequent to regeneration. In fact, he claimed that his life and ministry were forever changed as a result of this experience. It all began when two women in his church in Chicago set themselves to pray for him that he would receive this experience. As they prayed, his hunger for God increased until one day in 1871, he experienced God in a way that radically changed his life.

> I was crying all the time that God would fill me with His Spirit. Well, one day, in the city of New York--oh, what a day!--I cannot describe it, I seldom refer to it; it is almost too sacred an experience to name. Paul had an experience of which he never spoke for fourteen years. I can only say that God revealed Himself to me, and I had an experience of His love that I had to ask Him to stay His hand. I went to preaching again. The sermons were not different; I did not present any new truths, and yet hundreds were converted. I would not be placed back where I was before that blessed experience for all the world--it would be as the small dust of the balance.[24]

Although Moody's ministry was not generally character-ized by extraordinary manifestations of the Holy Spirit, such manifestations of the Holy Spirit as healing, prophecy and tongues were, indeed, not foreign to it. For example, his son recalls his father visiting the sick in Chicago and offering prayer "for the healing of both body and soul."[25] Another example comes from the testimony of Rev. R. Boyd, a Baptist minister, who went to a meeting where Moody had just spoken and was astounded by what he encountered. He recalls,

> When I got to the rooms of the Young Men's Christian Association, Victoria Hall, London, I found the meeting on fire. The young men were speaking with tongues, prophesying. What on earth did it mean? Only that Moody had addressed them that afternoon.[26]

## Rueben A. Torrey

Moody's associate and heir apparent, R. A. Torrey (1856-1928), popularized Moody's doctrine of Spirit baptism as a subsequent work of grace through Moody Bible Institute as well as through his speaking engagements and extensive writing projects. Torrey explicitly stated that "the baptism with the Holy Spirit is an operation of the Holy Spirit distinct from and subsequent and additional to his regenerating work."[27]

At one point, Torrey questioned whether it was necessary to speak in tongues in order to be baptized in the Holy Spirit. He finally concluded on the basis of 1 Corinthians 12:30 that it was not necessary, but he left the door open that it could occur. He says,

> It [Spirit baptism] is the impartation of supernatural power or gifts in service, and sometimes one may have rare gifts by the Spirit's power and few graces. . . . The power may be of one kind in one person and of another kind

in another person, but there will always be power."[28]

The doctrinal position of both Moody and Torrey concerning Spirit baptism would place them in the Charismatic camp had they lived in the second half of the twentieth century. Although Torrey reacted vehemently to the Pentecostal emphasis of tongues as the initial evidence of Spirit baptism, both he and Moody played a vital role in setting the stage for that movement through their emphasis on Spirit baptism and their openness to manifestations of the Spirit.

## Tongues and Pentecostal Language

Although speaking in tongues was not singled out as an important characteristic of the nineteenth century Holiness Revival, it did occur on occasion. In New England, for example, the Gift Adventists experienced speaking in tongues and the interpretation of tongues in their worship services.[29] In Cherokee County, North Carolina, during the summer of 1896, a revival resulted in numerous manifestations of spiritual gifts including healings and speaking in tongues.[30] This group later became the Church of God (Cleveland, TN).

Incidents such as these were usually accepted as simply additional manifestations of the Spirit in line with shouting, falling, and weeping. On the other hand, however, there were times, when speaking in tongues caused great consternation. A. M. Kiergan writes,

> One day right in the midst of a great sermon, a woman from Carrol County, a holiness professor, sprawled out at full length in the aisle. . . . Directly she began to compose a jargon of words in rhyme and sing them with a weird tune. She persisted till the service was spoiled and the camp was thrown into a hubbub. Strange to say, the camp was divided thereby. Some

said it was a wonderful manifestation of divine power, some said it was a repetition of speaking in unknown tongues as at Pentecost. But every preacher on the ground without exception declared it to be of the devil. But the camp was so divided in opinion that it had to be handled with the greatest of care.[31]

Regardless of the different views of speaking in tongues, by the final decade of the nineteenth century, Pentecostal language had permeated the entire Holiness Movement. Wesleyan scholar, Donald Dayton, points out that by this time, everything from campmeetings to choirs were being described as *Pentecostal*. Even personal experiences were being reported as *Pentecostal Testimonies.*[32]

This profusion of Pentecostal language and themes has been described by one writer as the attempt of the Holiness Revival "to restore primitive Christianity to the churches through a renewal of Pentecostal experience and an accompanying new age of the Holy Spirit."[33] This restorationist theme, along with the approach of the twentieth century, incited a new optimism among many believers concerning the future of the Church. Many felt that a new age of the Spirit was about to dawn that would restore primitive Christianity to the churches.[34]

Presbyterian minister, A. T. Pierson, expressed the prevailing mood when he said, "If in these degenerate days a new Pentecost would restore primitive faith, worship, unity, and activity, new displays of divine power might surpass those of any previous period."[35] Much of the Church, therefore, approached the twentieth century with what one writer has called "a spiritual expectancy unequaled in prior Protestant history."[36]

## Notes

[1] Charles Edward White, "Phoebe Palmer and the Development of Pentecostal Pneumatology." *Wesleyan Theological Journal*, Spring/Fall 1988: 208.

[2] Phoebe Palmer, *Four Years in the Old World* (Boston: Foster & Palmer, 1865), 145.

[3] Palmer, *Four Years in the Old World*, 145.

[4] Palmer, *Four Years in the Old World*, 120.

[5] Palmer, *Four Years in the Old World*, 103.

[6] Palmer, *Four Years in the Old World*, 111.

[7] Palmer, *Four Years in the Old World*, 107.

[8] Palmer, *Four Years in the Old World*, 107.

[9] Palmer, *Four Years in the Old World*, 127.

[10] Palmer, *Four Years in the Old World*, 96.

[11] Charles G. Finney, *An Autobiography* (Old Tappan: Revell, 1908), 20.

[12] Finney, 37.

[13] Finney, 161-162.

[14] V. Raymond Edman, *Finney Lives On* (Minneapolis: Bethany, 1971), 68.

[15] Finney, 55.

[16] See Chappell, 90-150.

[17] Dayton, "Christian Perfection to the Baptism of the Holy Ghost," 45. See also Frederick Dale Bruner, *A Theology of the Holy Spirit* (Grand Rapids: Eerdmans, 1970, 44-45, 340.

[18] A. J. Gordon, *The Ministry of the Holy Spirit* ((New York: Revell, 1895), 72.

[19] A. J. Gordon, *The Two-Fold Life* (Boston: Howard Garnett, 1884), 75-76.

[20] Gordon, *Healing*, 53.

[21] Gordon, *Healing*, 102-103.

[22] See Charles Parham, *The Everlasting Gospel* (Baxter Springs, KS: Apostolic Faith, n.d.), 74-76 for a chapter entitled "The Sealing." See also Gordon, *The Two-Fold Life*, 65-96 which is a chapter called "Salvation and Sealing." See also Gordon, *The Ministry of the Holy Spirit*, 77-82 where he again discusses the "sealing" of the Holy Spirit.

[23] Carl Brumback, *Like A River* (Springfield: Gospel Publishing, 1977), 79.

[24] William R. Moody, *The Life of D. L. Moody* (New York: Revell, 1900), 149.

[25] Moody, 127.

[26] Gordon Lindsay, "The Speaking in Tongues in Church History" *Voice of Healing*, August 1964: 3

[27] R. A. Torrey, *What The Bible Teaches* (n.p. Revell, 1898-1933), 271.

[28] Torrey, 273,275.

[29] Stanley H. Frodsham, *With Signs Following* (Gospel Publishing: Springfield, 1928), 333.

[30] Stanley M. Burgess and Gary B. McGee, ed., *Dictionary of Pentecostal and Charismatic Movements* (Grand Rapids: Zondervan, 1988), 198.

[31] A. M. Kiergan, *Historical Sketches of the Revival of True Holiness and Local Church Polity from 1865-1916* (Fort Scott, KS: Board of Publication of the Church Advocate and Good Way, 1971), 31; cited by Donald W. Dayton, "Christian Perfection to the Baptism in the Holy Ghost," 52.

[32] Dayton, "Christian Perfection to the Baptism in the Holy Ghost," 47.

[33] Melvin Dieter, "Wesleyan-Holiness Aspects of Pentecostal Origins," *Aspects of Pentecostal-Charismatic Origins*, ed. Vinson Synan (Plainfield: Logos, 1975), 58.

[34] Dieter, "Wesleyan-Holiness Aspects of Pentecostal Origins," 67.

[35] Arthur T. Pierson, *Forward Movements of the Last Half Century* (New York: Funk and Wagnalls, 1905), 401.

[36] Dieter, "Wesleyan-Holiness Aspects of Pentecostal Origins," 58.

CHAPTER 21

# Charles Fox Parham
# and Bethel Bible College

THE TWENTIETH CENTURY DAWNED with many standing on tiptoe, as it were, in expectation of what God was about to do. No one was more expectant than Charles Fox Parham (1873-1929), a young, itinerant evangelist with Methodist, Holiness, and Quaker influences. Parham's focus was world evangelism, but in his opinion, the Church of his day lacked the power necessary to fulfil the mandate of the Great Commission. He yearned for that outpouring from heaven that would make the Church a dynamic force in the earth, both in word and in deed.

### Seeking

In 1900, motivated by a desire to know more fully what others were experiencing, Parham traveled from his base in Topeka, Kansas, to various well-known ministries in the north and northeast. Among those that he visited were John Alexander Dowie's work in Chicago, Malone's *God's Bible School* in Cincinnati, Stephen Merritt's center in New York City, A. B. Simpson's work in Nyack, New York, A. J. Gordon's work in Boston, and Frank Sanford's *Holy Ghost and Us Bible School* near Durham, Maine. Evaluating his study tour, Parham remarks,

I returned home fully convinced that while many had

obtained real experience in sanctification and the anointing that abideth, there still remained a great outpouring of power for the Christians who were to close this age.[1]

## Bethel in Topeka, Kansas

In October, 1900, together with his Quaker wife and sister-in-law, Sarah and Lilian Thistlethwaite, Parham opened Bethel Bible College in Topeka, Kansas. About forty students attended, many of whom were already involved in some aspect of ministry. Bethel required no tuition; instead, the residents banned together to form a faith community in which they sought God's provision corporately through prayer and service. Their purpose was to "obey and live the commandments of Jesus."[2] Prayer was the central focus of the school, and the prayer tower atop the mansion was in use twenty-four hours with each resident of the school participating in a prayer vigil.

At the dedication of Bethel, one of the students, Captain Tuttle, saw a vision. Hovering over the school, was, as it were, a great body of water about to overflow. He understood this to mean that the outpouring of the Spirit about to occur at this school would be so abundant as to quench every spiritually thirsty soul on earth.

By late December, the students had completed their scheduled courses. Three days prior to New Year's Eve, 1900, Parham was scheduled to preach in Kansas City. Before leaving, he exhorted the students to study the subject of the baptism of the Holy Spirit, especially in the book of Acts. He urged them to search for objective, biblical evidence whereby a person could know for certain that he or she had truly received the baptism of the Holy Spirit. When he returned on

New Years Eve, Parham called the students together and inquired concerning their study.

> To my astonishment they all had the same story, that
> while there were different things occurred when the
> Pentecostal blessing fell, that the indisputable proof on
> each occasion was that they spoke with other tongues.[3]

## The Outpouring

In the Watchnight Service (1900-1901) later that evening,
the Holy Spirit manifested Himself with unusual intensity. At
about 11:00 p.m., as the twentieth century was about to
dawn, Agnes Ozman (1870-1937), a Holiness preacher who
was a student at the school, asked Parham to pray for her that
she might receive the baptism of the Holy Spirit in the manner they had observed in their study. Hesitant at first, he finally consented.

> Humbly in the name of Jesus, I laid my hand upon her
> head and prayed. I had scarcely repeated three dozen
> sentences when a glory fell upon her, a halo seemed to
> surround her head and face, and she began speaking in
> the Chinese language, and was unable to speak in Eng-
> lish for three days.[4]

This event fanned the flames of spiritual desire in Parham
and the others at Bethel. Suspending normal activities, they
set aside an upper room where they waited on the Lord for
their personal *Pentecost*. On January 3, while they continued
to pray, Parham went to preach at the Free Methodist
Church in Topeka. Sharing with the congregation the recent
events at Bethel, he predicted that when he returned that evening, the entire school would have received the Pentecostal
experience.

Parham arrived back at Bethel at about 10 p.m. and immediately mounted the stairs to the room where the others were
waiting on God. According to Parham, as he reached the top
of the stairs, he could see a sheen of light, brighter than the
light from the coal oil lamps, coming from the room. As he
entered the room, he was overwhelmed by what he encountered. Some were standing and others were kneeling. Together, in perfect harmony as if led by an invisible conductor,
they were singing *Jesus Lover of My Soul* in tongues. Sister
Stanley, one of the more mature students, approached him,
saying, "Just before you entered tongues of fire were sitting
above their heads."[5]

Finding his own place of prayer behind a table, Parham
knelt and asked God to give him this Pentecostal blessing. His
answer? If he were willing to withstand the persecutions,
hardships, trials, slander, and scandal it would entail, the full
blessing would be his. Parham replied, "Lord, I will. Just give
me this blessing."

> Right then there came a slight twist in my throat, a
> glory fell over me and I began to worship God in the
> Swedish tongue, which later changed to other languages
> and continued so until the morning.[6]

In the days and weeks that followed, various sincere seek-
ers and the curious arrived to investigate the bizarre events at
Bethel. Some received the baptism and took the message to
others. Throughout the spring, Parham and some of the students who remained at Bethel, continued to hold evangelistic
outreaches in nearby communities. Immediate results were
marginal, although one woman who received the baptism in
meetings at Lawrence, Kansas, carried the message to Des
Moines, Iowa, and Zion City, Illinois. She thus laid the foun-

dation for Parham's significant Pentecostal Revival in Zion City in 1906.

By summer, the mansion they were renting was sold and the residents dispersed. Sarah Parham notes, "Bethel Bible College was not intended to be a permanent school. The whole idea was a period of intensive training in the Word, prayer, and evangelism."[7] Indeed, it had served its purpose well.

## The Signficance of Bethel

The significance of Bethel Bible College was the students' articulation of speaking in tongues as the biblical evidence of Spirit baptism. Until this time, particularly in the nineteenth century Holiness Revival, speculation abounded concerning the actual biblical evidence of Spirit baptism. Although the doctrine was new to the Church-at-large, in certain respects, it was not without historical precedent. In the fourth and fifth centuries, both Augustine and Chrysostom had reached the same conclusion.[8] Unlike Parham and the students at Bethel, however, both had concluded that this pattern was intended for the first-century Church only.

In addition, seventy years prior to this time, the Scottish pastor, Edward Irving, as a result of his intense study of the New Testament, had reached the same conclusion as the students at Bethel. He had identified speaking in tongues as the "introductory sign" of Spirit baptism, noting that, biblically, tongues was the "gift first bestowed upon the baptized."[9]

For the twentieth century Church, however, the formulation of this doctrine was monumental. It offered the seeker objective criteria by which to determine when the experience of Spirit baptism had been received. It became a standard feature of Pentecostal doctrine and the distinguishing characteristic of the movement. Pentecostal pioneer J. Roswell Flower has said, "It was this decision [of tongues as evidence of Spirit baptism] which has made the Pentecostal Movement of the twentieth century.[10]

---

## Notes

[1] Sarah Parham, *The Life of Charles F. Parham* (Baxter Springs, KS: Apostolic Faith Bible College, 1930), 48.

[2] Charles F. Parham, *A Voice Crying in the Wilderness* (Baxter Springs, KS: Apostolic Faith, n.d.), 32.

[3] Sarah Parham, 52.

[4] S. Parham, 52.

[5] S. Parham, 53.

[6] S. Parham, 54.

[7] Carl Brumback, *A Sound from Heaven*, (Springfield: Gospel Publishing, 1977), 20.

[8] See Augustine, *The Epistle of Saint John*, 497-498 where he says, "In the earliest times, the Holy Ghost fell upon them that believed: and they spake with tongues which they had not learned." Augustine then continues this discussion and clearly demonstrates his view that, in the first century Church, the believer was expected to speak in tongues upon reception of the Holy Spirit. See also Chrysostom, *Homilies on First Corinthians*, 168 where Chrysostom, speaking of the first century Church, says, "Whoever was baptized he straightway spake with tongues . . . . And one straightway spake in Persian, another in Roman, another in Indian, another in some other tongue: and this made manifest to them that were without that it is the Spirit in the very person speaking."

[9] David Dorries, "Edward Irving and the Standing Sign," *Initial Evidence*, Gary B. McGee, Ed. (Peabody, MA: Hendrickson, 1991), 49.

[10] J. Roswell Flower, "Birth of the Pentecostal Movement" *Pentecostal Evangel*, 26 Nov. 1950: 3.

# CHAPTER 22

# William Seymour and the Azusa Street Revival

IN 1905, Parham went to Houston, Texas, where he conducted a successful revival campaign in Bryan Hall. The local newspaper carried reports of the many healings and other charismatic phenomena occurring in the meetings. To preserve the fruit of the revival and to prepare workers to carry the Pentecostal message throughout South Texas, Parham opened a short-term Bible school on January 1, 1906.

Although a number of important early Pentecostal leaders emerged from this campaign, perhaps the most famous was William Joseph Seymour (1870-1922), the pastor of a local, black Holiness congregation. He was especially intrigued by the doctrine of Spirit baptism evidenced by speaking in tongues which he heard that Parham was teaching.

When Seymour learned that Parham would be remaining in Houston and opening a short-term Bible school, he applied for enrollment. Because of southern segregation laws and customs, his application posed a problem. Parham, nonetheless, skirted the legal restrictions by arranging for Seymour to sit in an adjoining room where, through an open door, he was able to listen to the lectures. Although Seymour did not receive the experience of the baptism while at the school, he accepted it as biblically correct.

Seymour was consumed with a passionate desire for God.

Before I met Parham, such a hunger to have more of
God was in my heart that I prayed for five hours a day
for two and a half years. I got to Los Angeles, and there
the hunger was not less but more. I prayed, "God, what
can I do?" The Spirit said, "Pray more." "But Lord, I
am praying five hours a day now." I increased my
hours of prayer to seven, and prayed on for a year and
a half more. I prayed to God to give what Parham
preached, the real Holy Ghost and fire with tongues
with love and power of God like the apostles had.[1]

## The Call to Los Angeles

Before the courses were complete, Seymour received a letter from Los Angeles inviting him to pastor a newly formed
Holiness congregation. Having prayed about the opportunity,
he decided to accept. Parham provided his train fare and
blessed him as he departed around the middle of February.

In Los Angeles, Seymour preached his first sermon from
Acts 2:4 and broached the subject of tongues as the biblical
evidence of Spirit baptism. When he returned for the evening
service, he found the door padlocked. Church officials had
found his message of Spirit baptism evidenced by speaking in
tongues unacceptable.

The Asberrys, who lived on Bonnie Bray Street, then invited Seymour to their home where he gave himself to prayer
almost constantly. While eating supper one evening during
this time, Richard Asberry suddenly fell from his chair onto
the floor and began speaking in tongues. Soon others, including Seymour, were also experiencing the baptism in the Holy
Spirit and speaking in tongues.

As word spread that charismatic gifts were occurring on
Bonnie Bay Street, large crowds converged on the Asberry
residence. Forced to seek larger facilities, they found an

empty building at 312 Azusa Street in downtown Los Angeles. Formerly, it had been a Methodist Episcopal Church, but more recently it had been used as a stable and warehouse. They removed the debris and installed rough plank benches and a makeshift pulpit made from wooden shoe boxes. On April 14, 1906, they held their first service and revival fires blazed even more brightly.

## Prayer

Prayer seems to have been the foremost activity at the Azusa Mission. One participant said, "The whole place was steeped in prayer."[2] Seymour spent much of his time behind the pulpit with his head inside the top shoe box praying. An unpretentious man, he recognized his own need for the continual guidance and strength of the Holy Spirit. A contemporary, John G. Lake, described him as a man of great spiritual power. He says,

> God had put such a hunger into that man's heart that when the fire of God came it glorified him. I do not believe any other man in modern times had a more wonderful deluge of God in his life than God gave to that dear fellow, and the glory and power of a real Pentecost swept the world. That black man preached to my congregation of ten thousand people when the glory and power of God was upon his spirit, and men shook and trembled and cried to God. God was in him.[3]

## Holy Spirit Leadership

The services at Azusa were spontaneous. There were no pre-announced events, no special choirs, singers, or well-known evangelists. The services would usually begin around mid-morning and continue until three or four the following morning. One participant gives this description of a typical service.

> Someone might be speaking. Suddenly the Spirit would
> fall upon the congregation. God Himself would give
> the altar call. Men would fall all over the house, like the
> slain in battle, or rush for the altar *enmasse* to seek
> God. Presumptuous men would sometimes come
> among us. Especially preachers who would try to
> spread themselves in self-opinionation. But their effort
> was short lived. Their minds would wander, their
> brains reel. Things would turn black before their eyes.
> They could not go on. We simply prayed. The Holy
> Ghost did the rest.[4]

As services continued at the Azusa St. Mission, word
spread by word of mouth and newspapers that God was doing
a unique work there. *The Los Angeles Times* gave local coverage which, although it was not always positive, caught the
attention of the local populace. Frank Bartleman, a Holiness
journalist who participated in the revival, wrote articles about
the revival and sent them to Holiness publications throughout the country. Seymour also started a paper called *The Apostolic Faith* which soon reached a distribution of 50,000 copies.

News of the revival raised interest everywhere it reached
and soon the faithful and the curious were journeying from
far and near to experience the event. Thousands who were
hungry for a new outpouring of God's Spirit were baptized in
the Spirit and spoke in tongues. They came from across the
United States and Canada. Missionaries on foreign soil heard
of the revival and came. Visitors claimed that they could feel a
supernatural atmosphere within several blocks of the mission.[5] Multitudes received the Pentecostal experience and
went forth with new zeal, fresh vision, and increased Spirit-
empowerment for evangelism.

One of those whose life was transformed at the Azusa Mission was Ernest S. Williams who later served as general superintendent of the Assemblies of God (1929-1949). He first visited the revival in 1907 and was astounded by what he encountered.

> I wish I could describe what I saw. Prayer and worship were everywhere. The altar area was filled with seekers; some were kneeling; others were prone on the floor; some were speaking in tongues. Everyone was doing something; all were seemingly lost in God. I simply stood and looked, for I had never seen anything like it.[6]

Shortly thereafter, Williams received his personal Pentecost and spoke in tongues. Almost sixty years later, he revealed that that initial encounter with the Holy Spirit had not remained a unique experience.

> Soon it will be 59 years since I was filled with the Holy Spirit. I still have my seasons of refreshing from the presence of the Lord, speaking in other tongues and at times shaking under the influence of the Holy Spirit.[7]

## Interracial Character

The Azusa Mission reflected the original interracial nature that had chacterized the Pentecostal Revival from the beginning. The Parhams, from their home in the free-state of Kansas and with their strong Quaker perspectives, had always practiced both gender and racial equality. In Baxter Springs, Kansas, the Parhams ministered often in the local black Holiness church.[8] In segregated Texas, Parham found a means to skirt the *Jim Crow laws* and local customs in order for Seymour to attend the Houston Bible school. He also promoted a black, woman minister named Lucy Farrow who preached at his Houston campmeeting in August, 1906, and who demonstrated "an unusual power to lay hands on people for the reception of the Holy Spirit."[9] Robert Mapes Anderson says,

> Even before the Los Angeles revival, Parham had tapped this new ethnically heterogeneous constituency in Houston, where he garnered black converts like Seymour, Miss Farrow, and "Brother" Johnson, and some Mexican-Americans. At the 1913 summer encampment of Parham's group in Baxter Springs, Kansas, "White people, colored people and Indians all took part in the meeting and as Brother Parham remarked, 'We had the Gospel in black and white and red all over." For years, Parham held integrated meetings throughout the lower Midwest.[10]

When the revival broke out at Azusa, this concept of gender and racial equality continued. Bartleman said, "The color line was washed away in the blood."[11] The original Azusa board of directors consisted of seven women and three men. Five of the women were white and two were black. Of the three men, two were white and one, Pastor Seymour, was black.

### A Worldwide Phenomenon

The revival continued unabated for about three years (1906-1909). During this period, the Azusa St. Mission was a key instrument in dispersing Pentecostalism around the world. Ultimately, however, strife dampened the flames of revival and, as it smoldered, many whites left to begin their own churches and missions. By 1914, the Azusa Street Mission had become a small, local, black congregation.

Seymour continued as the senior pastor until his death on September 28, 1922, in Los Angeles. His wife then served as pastor until her death in 1936. Eventually, the mission was sold and was torn down to make room for a parking lot.

Seymour and Azusa Street, however, had carved for themselves a prominent place in the modern Pentecostal/Charismatic Movement. God used them as a catalyst to help spread the Pentecostal message around the world.

---

### Notes

[1] John G. Lake, *Spiritual Hunger/The God-Men* (Dallas: Christ for the Nations, 1980), 13.

[2] Frank Bartleman, *Azusa Street,* ed. Vinson Synan. (Plainfield: Logos, 1980), 60.

[3] Lake, *Spiritual Hunger/The God-Men*, 14.

[4] Bartleman, 59-60.

[5] Synan, 109.

[6] Ernest S. Williams, "Memories of Azusa Street Mission," Pentecostal Vertical File, Holy Spirit Research Center Oral Roberts University, 1.

[7] Williams, 1.

[8] Pauline Parham, Interview with author, May 14, 1995.

[9] B. F. Lawrence, The Apostolic Faith Restored (St. Louis: Gospel Publ., 1916), 66.

[10] Robert Mapes Anderson, *Vision of the Disinherited* (New York: Oxford, 1979), 123.

[11] Bartleman, 54.

CHAPTER 23

# Parham and
# the Zion City Revival

IN MAY 1906, Parham moved from Texas back to Kansas making his headquarters in the town of Baxter Springs. In September, he held a campmeeting at the city park with several hundred in attendance. At the time, in hand were two letters asking him for immediate help. One was from Seymour requesting that he travel to Los Angeles and help him with certain aspects of the meetings at the Azusa St. Mission.[1] The other was from friends in Zion City, Illinois, appealing to him to bring the Pentecostal message there. News of turbulent times in Zion City, together with an inner witness, prompted him to go north instead of west. He arrived in Zion City with several workers around mid-September.

### Trouble in Zion City

Zion City had been established by John Alexander Dowie in 1901 on the shores of Lake Michigan about forty miles north of Chicago. Dowie, known for his dramatic healing ministry, envisioned Zion as a Christian city from which missionaries would go forth to the ends of the earth. Ardent believers from many different parts of the nation relocated to Zion City with the dream of living in a Christian utopia.

Their dreams were crushed when, in 1906, political strife and financial mismanagement plunged the city into corporate bankruptcy. As Dowie and one of his lieutenants, Wilbur Voliva, jockeyed for political control of the city, the people sank into utter despair. The battle was finally taken to the federal courts where a federal judge turned over all of Zion's industries to the control of a receiver and ordered an election to choose an overseer for the city. Dowie encouraged his followers to boycott the election; consequently, Voliva received an overwhelming majority of the votes. The election did little to calm the turbulent emotions of the city's populace, many of whom had lost their life savings. A dark cloud of confusion, anger, bitterness, and strife seemed to hang over the city.

It was into this tumultuous atmosphere that Parham arrived with his small band of workers. Zion's impressive hotel, the Elijah Hospice, the largest wooden structure in the world at the time, initially served as headquarters for his meetings. The manager of the hospice, George H. Rogers, welcomed Parham and opened a large basement room where he and his workers held a meeting on the night they arrived. News of the meeting spread, and on the second night, the crowds filled two rooms and spilled over into the hallway. By the end of the week, they were conducting three services a day with hundreds attending.

### "'Til kingdom come."

Voliva, still struggling to consolidate his control of the city, was not at all pleased with Parham's success. The newspapers reported that he phoned Parham inquiring how long he planned to remain in Zion. Parham replied, "'Til kingdom come."[2] Since the Elijah Hospice was under city control, Voliva was able to oust Parham from those facilities. He then proceeded to rent every auditorium in the city so that Parham would not have a place for his meetings.

Not to be outdone, Parham responded by scheduling meetings in various homes throughout the city. With the assistance of his workers, he not only conducted meetings during the day but he also held five meetings concurrently every evening from 7 until midnight. He would hurry from one meeting to the next in a horse-drawn buggy and so was able to preach in each meeting during the evening.

The crowds increased, filling each home and overflowing onto the porches and lawns. According to the September 28, 1906, edition of *The Daily Sun* of Waukegan, Illinois, thousands were attending the meetings. Hundreds experienced release from bitterness, despair, and anger, and were baptized in the Holy Spirit. They saw visions, and hundreds responded to the call to full-time ministry. The fire of revival lifted them out of the fire of despair.

## The Divine Healing Connection

One of the most important, yet often overlooked results of Parham's Zion City Revival, was the permanent merger of the message of Divine healing in the Atonement[3] with the Pentecostal message. One of the cardinal teachings of Dowie and Zion City was Divine healing. Even before Parham's arrival with his message of Pentecost, Dowie and other residents of Zion City, such as John G. Lake, had carried on a successful ministry of Divine healing. Because Parham also operated in a significant healing ministry, and particularly through his ministry in Zion City, the two essential doctrines were permanently associated. Because Parham so ably combined the doctrines of divine healing and Spirit baptism, several independent healing evangelists emerged from his Zion City Revival.

## Laborers Thrust into the Harvest

Parham's work in Zion City not only opened the world-wide network of Christian Catholic Churches to the Pentecostal message, but also thrust at least five hundred consecrated and now Spirit-baptized ministers into the international harvest field.[4] In fact, some of the most productive and dynamic leaders of the Pentecostal Movement emerged from this revival. Tried, as it were, by fire during Zion's darkest hour, they had arisen from the ash heap of despair with renewed hope, restored vision for evangelism, and a new dimension of Holy Spirit power with which to fulfill that vision. Church historian, Paul G. Chappell reports,

> As a result of Parham's ministry in Zion City, several churches, a large faith home, a missionary training school were all established within the city limits and all advocated the pentecostal message. In addition, as Parham traveled to different branches of the Christian Catholic Church throughout America and Canada, he was able to convert them to the pentecostal doctrine. Some of Parham's Zion followers were responsible for spreading the message by traveling throughout the world, planting the pentecostal message in different countries such as South Africa, Australia, Switzerland, Holland, Jamaica, and India.[5]

Some of the more familiar names emerging from Zion City, to name only a few, include Cyrus Fockler, D. C. O. Opperman, Fred Volger, F. A. Graves, L. C. Hall and Martha Wing Robinson, Fred Hornshuh, Sr., Harry and Maggie Cantel, and Dr. Lilian B. Yeomans.[6] Fockler founded the Milwaukee Gospel Tabernacle; and Opperman, after leaving his position as superintendent of schools in Zion, joined the Apostolic Faith in Texas. Both of these men were among the founders of the Assemblies of God and served on its first executive presbytery. Volger served as assistant general superintendent of that same denomination for over fourteen years.[7] Fred Hornshuh, Sr. was one of the founders of the Open Bible Standard Churches, Lighthouse Temple in Eugene, Oregon, and Eugene Bible College.[8] Martha Wing Robinson founded the Zion Faith Homes. Dr. Lilian B. Yeomans was well known for her teaching and healing ministry. Harry Cantel, overseer of Dowie's Christian Catholic Church in England, visited Zion in 1907, was baptized in the Spirit, and returned to London with the Pentecostal message.

> Although others in England had received the baptism of the Spirit, and some prayer meetings had been held in a private home in London, this was the first "official" Pentecostal assembly in London. Also Highbury Missionary Guest House. It was in this home that the first Pentecostal wedding in England was held October 11, 1911, when Alice Rowlands and Stanley H. Frodsham were united by Smith Wigglesworth. In 1912, Mrs. Cantel moved to larger quarters known as Maranatha–one of the best known and best loved Pentecostal centers not only in London, but for the whole British Isles.[9]

Other Zion converts who became influential in the movement include E. N. Richey and his son Raymond T., who became known for his dynamic healing ministry.[10] In addition, perhaps three should be considered more closely: Marie Burgess Brown, F. F. Bosworth, and John G. Lake.

### Marie Burgess Brown

Marie Burgess Brown (1880-1971), a graduate of Moody Bible Institute, had moved to Zion where she had become a demonstrator of Zion manufactured goods in Chicago. She

lost her job when city officials learned that she was attending
the Parham meetings. She received her Spirit baptism on October 18, 1906, in one of Parham's meetings in the home of F.
F. Bosworth. Interestingly, both Bosworth and John G. Lake
were also baptized in the Spirit in that same home meeting.[11]
Years later, Brown recalled the event. She writes,

> I remember October 18, 1906 when the Lord baptized
> me in the Holy Spirit. For six hours He moved upon
> me in intercessory prayer for various mission fields.
> First He took me to China. I saw high stone walls and
> from beyond them heard the Chinese crying for help.
> As I prayed, it seemed stone after stone came out of the
> walls, and I saw a great multitude of Chinese waiting to
> hear the message of salvation. Then the Lord took me
> to India. There I saw the people of different castes, and
> I wondered and wept. But even as I wept for India's
> lost, the Lord showed me the continent of Africa. I
> preached to those people and they were especially re-
> sponsive. Then in a vision I went to Japan. There I en-
> tered an orphanage, and one by one the children came
> to me.[12]

Brown assumed that God was calling her to one of these
nations as a missionary. Parham, however, encouraged her to
go to New York City to minister, and there she founded and
pastored Glad Tidings Tabernacle which became one of the
most prominent Pentecostal churches in the nation. It became
a strong missionary church eventually sending missionaries to
every nation Brown had seen in the vision that October
night. In 1961, while she was still pastor, Glad Tidings Tabernacle was described as "a church with the largest missionary
budget in the missionary-minded Assemblies of God."[13]

## F. F. Bosworth

Another dynamic leader of the early Pentecostal movement who came out of the Zion City revival was F. F. Bosworth (1877-1958). During the revival, his home became
known as *Central Tabernacle*. After helping to nurture the
revival for a time, he launched into an international ministry
of faith and healing. His audiences in North America num-
bered as high as 20,000, and it has been estimated that over a
million souls were converted through his ministry.[14] He
authored the classic text, *Christ the Healer*, which is still used
around the world, and his influence reached into the 1950s
through his work with William Branham, Drs. T. L. and
Daisy Osborn, and other healing evangelists.

## John G. Lake

Dr. John G. Lake (1870-1935), a successful businessman
and resident in Zion City, emerged from the Zion City Revival as a giant firebrand in the Pentecostal Movement.[15]
Shortly after receiving his Spirit baptism, he gave away all his
possessions and launched into a ministry of faith. In South
Africa, his ministry ignited a revival characterized by remarkable healings and miracles. The movement he founded endured and today the Apostolic Faith of South Africa com-
prises over 2,500 churches. Interestingly, David du Plessis,
known as *Mr. Pentecost*, was converted and nurtured in an
Apostolic Faith Church of South Africa.

Lake also established several churches on the west coast of
the United States. In 1923, while pastoring in Portland, Oregon, he invited Parham to hold an evangelistic crusade. During one service, Gordon Lindsay (1906-73), who had been
born in Zion City, was converted. Lindsay's ministry, together with that of his wife Freda (1914- ), spanned the Pente-

costal, Healing, and Charismatic Revivals, and through Christ for the Nations in Dallas, Texas, is still highly influential.

## Conclusion

Both the Azusa and Zion City Revivals deserve important recognition for their respective roles in the Pentecostal Revival. In evaluating the influence of each, Chappell makes an astute observation. He concludes,

> The influence of the Azusa Street Revival tended to be focused upon bringing existing holiness churches into the new Pentecostal movement, whereas the Zion City Revival did bring a large part of Dowie's worldwide following into the movement, its focus was upon founding new independent ministries and independent churches.[16]

In retrospect, perhaps the Pentecostal revival in Zion City has been somewhat overlooked and therefore underestimated. As Gardiner notes, "The circumstances of this event . . . were so unostentatious and insignificant at the time that no one would or could have imagined its results."[17] The large number of individuals with far-reaching influence, the corporate influence of the Christian Catholic Churches around the world, and the permanent linking of divine healing with Pentecostalism certainly vindicate Parham's decision in 1906 to go to Zion City. Indeed, as one writer has said, his decision to go to Zion City precipitated one of the most important religious events of the twentieth century.[18]

## Notes

[1] Sarah Parham, 154-156.

[2] Sarah Parham, 159.

[3] Chappell, 356.

[4] Charles Parham, "The Latter Rain," *The Apostolic Faith*, Aug. 1962:2.

[5] Paul G. Chappell "The Divine Healing Movement in America" (Ph.D. Diss., Drew Univ., 1983), 351.

[6] See Gardiner, "Out of Zion . . . Into All the World," *Bread of Life*, Oct. 1981 - June 1985.

[7] Chappell, 355.

[8] Gardiner, Oct. 1982: 5.

[9] Gardiner, July 1982: 7.

[10] Gardiner, June, July, Oct., Nov. 1983.

[11] Gardiner, Oct. 1981: 5.

[12] Marie E. Brown, "I Remember," *Pentecostal Evangel*, 15 March 1964: 20.

[13] Brumback, *A Sound From Heaven*, 73.

[14] Gardiner, Oct. 1981:6.

[15] Gardiner, Nov. 1981:12.

[16] Chappell, 356-57.

[17] Gardiner, Oct. 1981:3.

[18] Gardiner, Oct. 1981:3.

# CHAPTER 24

# The Message Spreads Around the World

FROM AROUND THE WORLD, reports poured in of dynamic encounters with the Holy Spirit. From Europe, India, Africa, South America, and many other diverse regions, came news from believers who were being baptized in the Holy Spirit and speaking in tongues for the first time. Early Pentecostals saw this as a spontaneous spiritual eruption orchestrated by the Holy Spirit and it strengthened their conviction that this was the latter rain outpouring of the Holy Spirit that would usher in the end of the age and the coming of Christ.

## India

Pandita Ramabai (1858-1920), a well-educated woman born of an upper caste, had become a Christian in the latter part of the nineteenth century. An astute scholar, she was recognized by the Sanskrit scholars of Calcutta University who had conferred upon her the distinguished titles of *Sarawati* and *Pandita*. She mastered seven languages and translated the Bible from the original Hebrew and Greek into Marathi, her mother tongue. In addition, she authored *The High Caste Hindu Woman* and *A Life of Christ*, as well as numerous tracts which were distributed throughout India.

During a severe famine in the region of India where she lived, Ramabai opened a home for girls. In this endeavor, she was totally dependent on God's provision, and prayer was truly her lifeline. In January, 1905, Ramabai began to speak about the need to seek God for revival. Before long, 550 people, mostly women and girls, were meeting twice daily, praying for revival and for an enduement of power. On June 30, Ramabai was teaching the girls from John 8 when suddenly the Holy Spirit fell as in the book of Acts. Everyone in the room began to weep and pray aloud. The revival had begun.

Ramabai suspended regular school activities giving the Holy Spirit free reign in their midst. At the outset, confession of sin and repentance dominated, but then came glad singing, wonderful praise, and joy-filled dancing. Some experienced visions and supernatural dreams. Many experienced the baptism in the Holy Spirit accompanied by speaking in tongues. A visitor to the school at this time was missionary Albert Norton who writes,

> One week ago I visited the Mukti Mission. Miss Abrams asked me if I should like to go into a room where about twenty girls were praying. After entering, I knelt with closed eyes by a table on one side. Presently I heard someone praying near me very distinctly in English. Among the petitions were "O Lord, open the mouth; O Lord open the mouth; O Lord, open the heart; O Lord, open the heart; O Lord open the eyes! O Lord, open the eyes! Oh, the blood of Jesus, the blood of Jesus! Oh, give complete victory! Oh, such a blessing! Oh, such glory!"
>
> I was struck with astonishment, as I knew that there was no one in the room who could speak English, beside Miss Abrams. I opened my eyes and within three feet of me, on her knees, with closed eyes and raised hands was a woman, whom I had baptized at Kedgaon in 1899, and whom my wife and I had known intimately since as a devoted Christian worker. Her

174

mother tongue was Marathi, and she could speak a little
Hindustani. But she was unable to speak or understand
English such as she was using. But when I heard her
speak English idiomatically, distinctly and fluently, I
was impressed as I should have been had I seen one,
whom I knew to be dead, raised to life. A few other illiterate Marathi women and girls were speaking in English and some were speaking in other languages which
none at Kedgaon understood. This was not gibberish,
but it closely resembled the speaking of foreign languages to which I had listened but did not understand.[1]

As Norton witnessed others being baptized in the Spirit
baptism and speaking in tongues, he was amazed to hear so
many speaking in English rather than one of the many languages of India. He had no clear answer but did offer a possible solution.

I have an idea that it is in mercy to us poor missionaries from Europe and America who, as a class, seem to
be Doubting Thomases, in regard to gifts and workings
of the Spirit, and not receiving the power of the Holy
Spirit as we ought.[2]

Pandita Ramabai left her imprint on her generation and
surely deserves to be recognized as the *Mother of the Pentecostal Movement* in India. According to a visitor to her mission,
she was "the most remarkable combination of executive, intellectual and religious powers that I know of in recent times
in either man or woman."[3] In recognition of her social impact
on the nation, the Government of India, in 1989, issued a
postage stamp in her honor.

## South America

In 1907, Minnie Abrams (1859-1912), who worked for a
time with Pandita Ramabai, sent an account of the Mukti re-

175

vival to her friends, Willis C. (1856-1936) and Mary Anne Hoover, Methodist missionaries to Chile. As they read their friend's eye-witness account of the remarkable outpouring of the Holy Spirit in India, they were stirred to seek God for a similar revival in Chile.

The Hoovers immediately instituted special prayer times among their congregation for the purpose of revival. It was not unusual for many to spend entire nights in prayer. Conviction of sin gripped the minds of the people. Many openly confessed their sin, while others made restitution for wrong-doing. But this, it seems, was preparatory for what was yet to come.

On July 4, 1909, the flood gates of heaven opened and revival broke forth with tremendous power. Hoover describes what happened.

> Saturday night was an all night of prayer, during which four vain young ladies (three of them were in the choir) fell to the floor under the power of the Spirit. One of them, after lying a long time, began to exhort saying, "The Lord is coming soon and commands us to get ready." The effect produced was indescribable. The following morning in Sunday School, at ten o'clock, a daze seemed to rest upon the people. Some were unable to rise after the opening prayer which had been like "the sound of many waters," and all were filled with wonder. From that time on the atmosphere seemed charged by the Holy Spirit, and people fell on the floor, or broke out in other tongues, or singing in the Spirit, in a way impossible in their natural condition. On one occasion a woman, a young lady, and a girl of twelve were lying on the floor in different parts of the prayer room, with eyes closed and silent. Suddenly, as with one voice, they burst forth into a song in a familiar tune but in unknown tongues, all speaking the same

words. After a verse or two they became silent; then again suddenly, another tune, a verse or two, and silence. This was repeated until they had sung ten tunes, always using the same words and keeping in perfect time together as if led by some invisible chorister.[4]

Needless to say, such bizarre events attracted public attention and the congregation exploded in growth as the curious, convicted, and convinced drew near.

Close on the heels of all of this came persecution as the local press leveled false and blatant charges against the Pentecostals. This seemed only to arouse more curiosity, however, and many who attended the meetings out of curiosity went away convinced that a genuine work of God was in progress. After two months, attendance had jumped from 300 to almost 1,000, and the revival was spreading to other cities.

In February, 1910, Hoover was forced by his superiors in the Methodist Church to choose between returning to America or leaving the Methodist Church if he were to remain as a missionary in Chile. He chose to leave the Methodist Church and to remain in Valparaiso. He and 440 followers found new facilities, and the Pentecostal revival mushroomed.

In view of these events, Hoover has been honored as *The Founder of Pentecostalism in Chile*. Today, in Chile, well over one million Pentecostals constitute various Pentecostal groups. The Pentecostal Methodist Church, founded by Hoover, now numbers over 600,000 members, while the Chilean Methodist Church which rejected the revival has shrunk to only 4,000 members. C. Peter Wagner has commented, "Many Methodists who blamed the devil for what happened in 1909 have since wondered out loud on whose side the devil might really have been."[5]

## Europe

T. B. Barratt (1862-1940) of Norway, a minister with the Methodist Episcopal Church, journeyed to America in 1906 to raise money for missions in Norway. Having arrived on the east coast, he was moved by reports coming from the Azusa Street Revival in Los Angeles. Immediately, he began to seek the baptism in the Holy Spirit, and on October 7, 1907, he received. He testifies that he spoke and sang by the power of the Spirit in several different languages.[6]

Barratt returned to Norway and began immediately to preach his new Pentecostal message. The results were phenomenal.

> Folk from all denominations are rushing to the meetings. A number have received their Pentecost and are speaking in tongues. Some have seen Jesus in our meetings, and tongues of fire have been seen over my head by an infidel, convincing him of the power of God. People who have attended the meetings are taking the fire with them to the towns round about.[7]

News of these events spread quickly and soon visitors journeyed to Oslo from other nations. At the peak of revival in 1907, A. A. Boddy (1854-1930), Anglican rector in Sunderland (1884-1922), England, visited. Boddy was seeking a greater dimension in his Christian experience and was convinced that what he saw in Norway was a genuine work of the Holy Spirit. When he returned to Sunderland, a Pentecostal revival broke out in his church and eventually spread throughout the British Isles. Sunderland, in fact, became a center of Pentecostal renewal visited by thousands. Among these was Smith Wigglesworth (1859-1947) who received his Spirit baptism when Mrs. Boddy laid hands on him and prayed. Wigglesworth, renowned for his ministry of faith and healing, preached and ministered in the gifts of the Spirit around the world.

## China

In China, Christian and Missionary Alliance missionary, William Simpson (1869-1961), learned of the Pentecostal revival in 1908. The first person he heard speak in tongues was his illiterate Chinese cook at a convention on the Tibetan border. The man went on to interpret the message in both Mandarin and local dialects. Intrigued by this experience, Simpson devoted four years of intense study and prayer concerning Spirit baptism and the gift of tongues. On May 5, 1912, he was baptized in the Spirit and spoke in tongues.

Simpson's acceptance of Pentecostal experience and doctrine necessitated his withdrawal from the Christian and Missionary Alliance. This, in turn, meant he no longer received his regular support from America. In spite of this hardship, he continued his work, and with the added dimension of charismatic power, the effectiveness of his efforts increased. Preaching the Pentecostal message, he saw many receive Spirit baptism accompanied by speaking in tongues. In addition, other charismatic phenomena, such as falling, visions, and healings, accompanied his ministry.

In 1915, Simpson and his family returned to the United States. They affiliated with the newly formed Assemblies of God, and in 1916, he accepted the post of principal of Bethel Bible Institute in Newark, New Jersey. He also served on the first Assemblies of God foreign missions committee and helped the organization develop its missions program.

Love for China, where he had already spent twenty years of his life, still dominated his heart. In 1918, an incident occurred that served to thrust Simpson back to his first love.

179

In a campmeeting the Spirit spoke just as directly to me as He had spoken long ago to Paul: It was in Chinese through a sister who knew not one word of Chinese and told me to go back to Taochow on the Tibetan border. So I was sent forth by the Holy Spirit, sailing again on February 4, 1918. The Lord opened the way until we reached the border, and as soon as we arrived on that mission field the Spirit of God was poured out . . .. We received letters inviting us here and there, and wherever we went the Spirit was poured out in Pentecostal power.[8]

## Proliferation

Reports poured in of other Pentecostal outpourings in Latin America, Africa, Europe, and the islands of the seas. The revival, without any organized agenda, was exploding in numbers and influence around the world. By 1908, the movement had taken root in over 50 nations. By 1914, it was represented in every American city of 3000 or more and in every area of the world from Iceland to Tanzania, and Pentecostals were publishing literature in 30 languages.[9]

---

### Notes

[1] Stanley H. Frodsham, *With Signs Following* (Springfield, MO: Gospel Publ., 1946), 107-108.

[2] Frodsham, *With Signs Following*, 108.

[3] *Dictionary of Pentecostal-Charismatic Movements*, 756.

[4] Frodsham, *With Signs Following*, 177-178.

[5] Vinson Synan, *In the Latter Days* (Ann Arbor: Servant, 1984), 60.

[6] Frodsham, *With Signs Following*, 71

[7] Frodsham, *With Signs Following*, 71-72.

[8] Edith Blumhofer, *Pentecost in My Soul*, (Springfield:GPH., 1989), 244.

[9] Douglas G. Nelson, "A Search for Pentecostal-Charismatic Roots," (Ph.D Diss., University of Birmingham, England, 1981), Synopsis.

CHAPTER 25

# Further Developments
# in Pentecostalism

### *The Latter Rain Covenant*

ONE OF THE EARLIEST defenses of Pentecostalism was David Wesley Myland's 1910 book, *The Latter Rain Covenant and Pentecostal Power*.[1] In this volume, Myland defended the Pentecostal revival as being the latter rain promised in both the Old and New Testaments. As such, it was destined to bring about a great harvest of souls and to usher in the end of the age.

Myland pointed out that the early and latter rain originally referred to the natural, seasonal rain cycle in Israel. When the Israelites had come out from Egypt into the land of their inheritance, God promised that if they would be faithful to love and serve Him, He would be faithful in sending the early and latter rains in their proper seasons. The result would be abundant harvests.[2]

The early rain came at the beginning of the growing season just after planting, causing the seeds to germinate and take root, and giving them a hearty start in their growth toward maturity. The latter rain came toward the end of the growing season maturing the crops for harvest. Between these two rainy seasons was a long dry period when only isolated, intermittent showers fell.

Later, certain Old Testament prophets began giving a spiritual application to the concept of the early and latter rain.[3] Hosea, for example, predicted a visitation of God to the earth and also told the manner in which He would come. He will come, Hosea said, "like the rain; like the early and the latter rain to the earth" (Hosea 6:3). Joel 2:23 also promises "the early and the latter rain," and the writer of Proverbs 16:15 says, God's "favor is as a cloud of the latter rain." Zechariah 10:1 says, "Ask for rain in the time of the latter rain."

The concept is carried over into the New Testament. James refers specifically to the early and latter rain and applies it to the church age and the coming of Christ. He says that Christ will come only after the earth has received both the early and latter rain and the resulting harvest.[4]

For Myland and his Pentecostal colleagues, the early and latter rain provided a paradigm through which to view the history of the Church from the Day of Pentecost to the present time. The early rain represented the outpouring of the Holy Spirit that began on the Day of Pentecost and continued unabated through the first century. Afterwards came the long, dry season when spiritual gifts were rare. The advent of the Pentecostal Revival, they insisted, was the latter rain outpouring of the Holy Spirit, and as such, it was a sign of the impending end of the age and return of Christ to the earth.

## A Trend Toward Denominationalism

By the second decade of the century, a trend toward denominationalism became obvious within the movement. As institutional distinctives in discipline and doctrine were defined, cooperation and fellowship based on the common experience of Spirit baptism became less common. The denominations usually formed along theological and racial lines. The Church of God in Christ, for example, organized in 1907 and now the largest Pentecostal denomination in America, was predominately a black denomination. The Assemblies of God, organized by white Pentecostals in 1914, was the first non-Wesleyan Pentecostal group. Oneness or unitarian Pentecostal groups began forming especially after 1916. Several Wesleyan-Holiness groups already in existence before 1900, such as the Church of God (Cleveland, TN) and the Pentecostal Holiness Church, had, in fact, become Pentecostal in doctrine and practice as early as 1906 through the overflow of the Azusa Street Revival.

These organizations continued to grow rapidly and by the 1940s were attracting the attention of the rest of the church world. At the founding meeting of the National Association of Evangelicals in 1942, ten percent of the delegates were Pentecostal. Although received warily at first, the Pentecostals eventually gained full acceptance in this evangelical organization and now constitute the majority of its membership.

Along with the growing acceptance of their movement, Pentecostals were, at the same time, experiencing a loss of spiritual vitality that always accompanies the onslaught of institutionalism. The 1930s and 40s have been described as a time when "the depth of worship and the operation of the gifts of the Spirit so much in evidence in earlier decades were not so prominent."[5] Many were concerned to the point that systematic times of prayer and fasting were instituted to pray for spiritual renewal and revival. The answer to their prayers began with the advent of the Healing Revival which began in 1946, and the Latter Rain Revival which began in 1947.

183

## Notes

[1] D. W. Myland, *The Latter Rain Covenant and Pentecostal Power* (Chicago: Evangel Publishing House, 1910).

[2] The Bible, Deut. 11:13-15.

[3] See The Bible, Hos. 6:3, Joel 2:23-24 and Zech. 10:1.

[4] The Bible, James 5:7.

[5] Carl Brumback, *Suddenly . . . From Heaven* (Springfield: Gospel Publ., 1962), 331.

# CHAPTER 26

# The Healing Revival

## William Branham

WILLIAM BRANHAM (1909-65), is normally recognized as the person God used to initiate the Healing Revival of the late forties and early fifties. When it all began, Branham, a Baptist minister in Jeffersonville, Indiana, was moonlighting as a game warden because the small church he was pastoring was unable to support him and his family. He was a humble man with a simple faith in the God of the Bible.

In 1946, Branham reported that an angel had appeared to him instructing him to carry a gift of healing to the world. According to Branham, the angel had appeared at 11 p.m on May 7, 1946, after a time of prayer, and said,

> Fear not. I am sent from the presence of Almighty God to tell you that your peculiar life and your misunderstood ways have been to indicate that God has sent you to take a gift of divine healing to the people of the world. If you will be sincere, and can get the people to believe you, nothing shall stand before your prayer, not even cancer.[1]

Branham immediately launched into a successful evangelistic and healing ministry but with limited exposure. Respecting Branham's potential, and valuing his wonderful gift, yet understanding his need for wise administration, Pastor Jack Moore, a Oneness Pentecostal from Shreveport, Louisiana, brought Branham together with Gordon Lindsay. Lindsay, who was well-known and highly respected in Pentecostal circles, agreed to serve as Branham's campaign manager. His ability to organize and garner support for city-wide campaigns thrust Branham into national and international prominence.

Branham operated in a particularly powerful ministry of the word of knowledge. When this gift manifested, he often revealed intimate details of the person's life to whom he was ministering. Through a gift of healing, he was also able to detect and diagnose disease by pulsations in his left hand which would occur when he would take the afflicted person's left hand.

Walter Hollenweger (1927-), Professor of Mission at the University of Birmingham, England, served as Branham's interpreter in Europe on several occasions. In his monumental work *The Pentecostals*, he says,

> The author, who knew Branham personally and interpreted for him in Zurich, is not aware of any case in which he was mistaken in the often detailed statements he made. It was characteristic of Branham's kindheartedness that he gave certain personal revelations to those who were seeking healing in a whisper, so that they could not be picked up by the microphone and revealed to the spectators.[2]

## Oral Roberts

About this same time, God was dealing with Oral Roberts, a young pastor in Enid, Oklahoma. A divinity student at Phillips University, Roberts was pastor of a small Pentecostal Holiness Church in Enid. In 1935, when he was seventeen, he had been miraculously healed of advanced tuberculosis. God had spoken to him at that time, saying, "I have called you to take my healing power to your generation." Now he was diligently seeking God for a fresh outpouring of the Holy Spirit in his own life and ministry and for the fulfillment of that word.

On May 14, 1947, following a seven month season of focused prayer and fasting, Roberts received inner assurance that it was time for God's call to begin to be fulfilled.[3] At this time, God also revealed to Roberts that he would feel His power in his right hand and that, as he laid his hands on the sick, he would be able to detect the name and number of any demons which might be present.

With this assurance fresh in his mind, he launched into a ministry which emphasized healing for the body and salvation for the soul. His ministry was an instant success. In 1948, to accommodate the crowds, he ordered a tent which would seat two thousand. The crowds continued to increase and by 1953, he was conducting meetings under a tent that seated 12,500. Many remarkable miracles occurred and Roberts eventually became the most prominent healing evangelist of that era.

## The Voice of Healing

The ministries of William Branham and Oral Roberts signaled the beginning of a significant era of healing evangelism. Almost immediately, a host of other evangelists began reporting miraculous healings and other supernatural phenomena in their meetings. These included A. A. Allen, Jack Coe, T. L. Osborn, William Freeman, W. V. Grant, Kenneth Hagin, and many other evangelists.

Lindsay, who separated from Branham in 1955, provided cohesion to the revival through his *Voice of Healing* magazine and annual *Voice of Healing* conventions. His magazine reported the revivals of various evangelists and served as a platform giving them national recognition. His efforts were also instrumental in launching the ministries of several prominent evangelists of this era. One writer has described Lindsay's role in the revival as "the conductor of an unruly orchestra."[4]

## T. L. and Daisy Osborn

In 1945, T. L. and Daisy Osborn (1923-  ; 1924-95) went to India as Pentecostal missionaries. Unable to persuade the teeming masses to believe in the Lord Jesus Christ, the young couple returned to America. They had seen the suffering masses without Christ, however, and because of that fact, they would not rest until they had found a way to reach them with the Gospel.

While pastoring in the northwest, they diligently sought God for the answer—and God rewards those who diligently seek Him (Heb. 11:6). As they began to hold evangelistic and healing crusades, God confirmed the Gospel with signs and wonders, and they knew they had found the answer for the masses such as they had seen in India. Following a period of cooperative ministry with the Voice of Healing in America, the Osborns returned to the mission fields of the world. Traveling to 76 nations, they pioneered mass healing crusades with phenomenal results. They found that demonstrations of God's compassion and healing power would result in thousands accepting Christ in a single service. Their huge outdoor crusades became the pattern for mass evangelism in developing nations. As they approached their seventies, it was said of this husband/wife team that they had preached the Gospel to more people, face-to-face, than anyone to that point in history.

## Conclusion

By the end of 1956, the Healing Revival was being rent by strife between the healing evangelists and the Pentecostal denominations to which they belonged. Some of the strife was simply jealousy on the part of the denominations, and some was due to questionable practices by some of the evangelists. The conflict resulted in the waning of the revival and a period of crisis for many of the healing revivalists. Some were not able to continue. Among the best known who successfully continued their ministries were Gordon and Freda Lindsay, who founded Christ For the Nations in Dallas, Texas; Oral Roberts, who founded Oral Roberts University in Tulsa, Oklahoma; T. L. and Daisy Osborn, who continued their multi-faceted missionary evangelism from Osborn Foundation International in Tulsa, Oklahoma; and Kenneth Hagin, who founded Rhema Bible Training Center in Broken Arrow, Oklahoma.

The Healing Revival provided an important link between the Pentecostal Movement and the Charismatic Renewal which began around 1960. As the Healing Revival waned, the Charismatic Renewal emerged to an even larger and more receptive audience. Several of those who had played prominent roles in the Healing Revival now became instrumental in the successes of the Charismatic Movement.

---

### Notes

[1] David Harrell Jr., *All Things are Possible* (Bloomington: Indiana Univ. Press, 1975), 28.

[2] Walter Hollanweger, *The Pentecostals* (Peabody, MA: Hendrickson, 1988), 354.

[3] Harrell, 42.

[4] Harrell, 57.

# CHAPTER 27

# The Latter Rain Revival

ALMOST PARALLEL with the post-war Healing Revival, and in a sense overlapping it, was another revival known as the Latter Rain Revival. It began among students and staff of Sharon Bible College in North Battleford, Saskatchewan, Canada, in February, 1948. From there, it spread rapidly throughout North America and around the world.[1]

### The Outpouring at Sharon Bible College

The revival began when teachers from Sharon Bible College in North Battleford, Saskatchewan, visited revival services conducted by William Branham in Vancouver, British Columbia, in the fall of 1947.[2] Deeply impressed by Branham's demonstration of the word of knowledge and by the miraculous healings which they observed, they and the students of Sharon began fasting, praying, and studying the Scriptures with heightened expectation. On February 12, 1948, they experienced an unusual demonstration of God's presence and power. Ern Hawtin, a faculty member at the time, describes what happened in the following account.

> Some students were under the power of God on the floor, others were kneeling in adoration and worship before the Lord. The anointing deepened until the awe of God was upon everyone. The Lord spoke to one of the brethren. "Go and lay hands upon a certain student and pray for him." While he was in doubt and contem-

191

plation one of the sisters who had been under the power of God went to the brother saying the same words, and naming the identical student he was to pray for. He went in obedience and a revelation was given concerning the student's life and future ministry. After this a long prophecy was given with minute details concerning the great thing God was about to do. The pattern for the revival and many details concerning it were given.[3]

The students spent the next day searching the Scriptures for insight and confirmation of the previous day's events. On February 14,

It seemed that all Heaven broke loose upon our souls, and heaven came down to greet us. Soon a visible manifestation of gifts was received when candidates were prayed over, and many as a result were healed, as gifts of healing were received.[4]

### The Signficance of Sharon

Historian Richard Riss, who has studied the Latter Rain extensively, maintains that the events at Sharon raised hope and interest particularly because a general dearth of manifestations had pervaded Pentecostalism between 1935 and 1947. The curious and the spiritually hungry flocked to North Battleford from across America and around the world. *The Sharon Star* carried reports and advertised campmeetings and conventions. Before long, Sharon faculty members were responding to invitations to minister throughout North America.[5]

### Increase and Opposition

The revival quickly garnered support. In January, 1949, Pentecostal pioneer, Stanley Frodsham (1882-1969), visited

Bethesda Missionary Temple in Detroit, Michigan, at the invitation of its pastor, Myrtle D. Beall (1896-1979). Beall had recently embraced the revival and wanted Frodsham to see the outpouring of the Spirit which her congregation was experiencing. Frodsham, ordained with the Assemblies of God and editor of the denomination's *Pentecostal Evangel*, was impressed by what he saw and became a supporter of the revival. A number of other well-known ministers also embraced the revival including: Reg Layzell of Glad Tidings Temple in Vancouver, British Columbia; Ivan and Minnie Spencer of Elim Bible Institute, Lima, New York; Zion Evangelistic Fellowship in Providence, Rhode Island; Lewi Pethrus of Sweden; and many others.[6]

With emphasis on the laying on of hands for the impartation of spiritual gifts, the recognition of apostles and prophets in the present day Church, and the gift of prophecy for directing and commissioning ministerial candidates and *proper* church government, the revival drew opposition. Although many of these practices had been common among early Pentecostals, they were rejected by most of the Pentecostal denominations.[7] As a result of the opposition, a number of ministers left their denominations, including Frodsham. Most of these worked as independent ministers or joined loosely formed fellowships. Although rejected by Pentecostal denominations, these Latter Rain believers continued and, to a degree, influenced and were absorbed into the Charismatic Renewal of the 1960s-70s.[8]

---

### Notes

[1] Richard Riss, "The New Order of the Latter Rain, A Look at the Revival Movement on Its 40th Anniversary," *Assemblies of God Heritage*, Fall 1987: 16.

[2] Riss, 15.

[3] Riss, 17.

[4] Riss, 17.

[5] Riss, 17

[6] Riss, 17.

[7] See Corum, *Like as of Fire*, Preface, p. 6 who states that the official board of twelve at Azusa Street would lay their hands on newly approved ministers and pray "as did the apostles of old. People were told where to go on the mission field through visions and prophecy and results followed wherever they went." See also Richard Riss, "The New Order of the Latter Rain," 16 who lists many of the similarities of the Latter Rain Movement with the older Pentecostal movement including the fact that both were known as the Latter Rain Movement.

[8] Riss, 17.

# CHAPTER 28

# The Charismatic Movement

## Dennis Bennett and the Protestant Renewal

THE APRIL 1960 ISSUE OF *TIME* carried the story of an Episcopal priest in Van Nuys, California, who had announced to his congregation that he had been baptized in the Holy Spirit and had spoken in tongues. Dennis Bennett (1917-1992), rector of St. Mark's Episcopal Church, had initially received this experience while praying in his home in November, 1959. Other news agencies, picking up the story from *Time*, gave it further coverage. Although others in the historic churches had experienced speaking in tongues prior to this, the event usually marks the beginning of the modern Charismatic Renewal.

Although Bennett had considerable support from within his parish, a small group vehemently denounced his Pentecostal activity. He resigned from St. Mark's under pressure and was assigned to the pastorate of St. Luke's Episcopal Church in Seattle, Washington. Regardless, the outpouring of the Holy Spirit had begun, and by 1963, *Christianity Today* estimated that 2000 Episcopalians in southern California were experiencing the charismatic phenomenon of speaking in tongues. Indeed, the *Charismatic* Renewal had begun.

In a sense, Bennett had been sent to the back side of the desert. St. Luke's was on the brink of extinction, having already been shut down twice. But an astounding thing happened. St. Luke's not only returned from the dead, but flourished, becoming one of the strongest churches in the North-

195

west. It became an important center of charismatic renewal, not only for Episcopalians, but also for many other denominations as Bennett and the congregation hosted and helped visiting clergy and laypersons from many denominations. As with most *Neo-Pentecostals* (as the early Charismatics were called) Bennett promoted speaking in tongues as the intitial Bible evidence of Spirit baptism.

Like a prairie fire fanned by the wind, Pentecost spread quickly, penetrating most of the historic Protestant denominations. Charismatic prayer groups sprang up across the country. In these informal gatherings, participants sang praises, prayed spontaneously, and unashamedly spoke and sang in tongues, and enthusiastically ministered to one another in the various gifts of the Holy Spirit.

Unlike the Pentecostals sixty years earlier, many of the Charismatics found acceptance in their denominations. In fact, the leaders of the movement saw the revival as God's way of renewing the existing denominations. For this reason, they encouraged the people to remain within their churches and, for the same reason, they preferred the word *renewal* instead of *revival* to describe what was happening .

## The Catholic Charismatic Movement

The groundwork for the Charismatic Movement in the Roman Catholic Church had been firmly laid by the Vatican II Council (1962-1965). Pope John XXIII, in calling the Council, expressed his desire for the dawning of a new Pentecost which he said "is the hope of our yearning."[1] He also directed the churches to pray that the Holy Spirit would renew His wonders "in this our day as by a new Pentecost."[2]

Vatican II's careful acceptance of those outside the Roman Catholic fold made possible new opportunities for interaction with Christians of other persuasions. Instead of using the harsh term *heretic*, which had been employed for centuries, it chose the phrase *separated brethren* in referring to non-Catholic Christians. It also declared that Christians of other denominations "are joined with us in the Holy Spirit, for to them also he gives his gifts and graces." These were important statements, since Christians from non-Catholic churches would become instrumental in leading many Roman Catholics into the baptism in the Holy Spirit.[3]

Of equal importance was the attitude taken by the Council concerning charismatic gifts. When the subject arose for discussion, Cardinal Ruffini expressed the traditional Roman Catholic view that such gifts today "are extremely rare and altogether exceptional."[4] Contrariwise, Cardinal Suenens pointed out that the charismatic dimension, according to St. Paul, is *necessary* to the Church. He went on to say that these gifts are "no peripheral or accidental phenomenon in the life of the Church;" on the contrary, he said, they are "of vital importance for the building up of the mystical body."[5] As a result of Cardinal Suenens' influence, the Council adopted an open and receptive position on the *charismata,* declaring that these gifts "should be recognized and esteemed in the Church of today."[6] With this foundation in place, as Vinson Synan (1934-), writes, "It was almost inevitable that *Pentecostalism* would break out in the Roman Catholic Church."[7]

It began with a retreat attended by about twenty professors and graduate students from Duquesne University in Pittsburgh, Pennsylvania, on the weekend of February 17-19, 1967. In preparation for the retreat, the participants were asked to read the book of Acts and David Wilkerson's *The Cross and the Switchblade.* When the group gathered in the chapel on Saturday evening, they experienced a mighty outpouring of the Holy Spirit and some began speaking in tongues. Synan says,

> As these Catholic seekers prayed through to Pentecost, many things familiar to classical Pentecostals began to take place. Some laughed uncontrollably "in the Spirit," while one young man rolled across the floor in ecstasy. Shouting praises to the Lord, weeping and speaking in tongues characterized this beginning of the movement in the Catholic Church.[8]

The Fire at Duquesne soon spread to Notre Dame University, the center of American Catholicism. Many of its professors and students received the baptism in the Holy Spirit and spoke in tongues. From there the movement spread rapidly with Catholic Charismatic prayer groups springing up across the country. By 1970, a Catholic Charismatic conference at Notre Dame attracted 30,000 Catholic Charismatics. Priests, nuns, and laypeople together sang and prayed in tongues, prophesied, and rejoiced in what God was doing.

## Ecumenism and Schisms

Because of the ecumenical character of the Renewal, extensive cross pollination occurred. Conferences were the order of the day, and conference participants normally represented a healthy cross section of Christendom. Catholic priest and scholar, Peter Hocken (1932-), has referred to the movement as "an ecumenical gift of grace poured out on all the churches."[9]

The highwater mark of the renewal occurred in 1977 when 52,000 Pentecostal/Charismatics met in Arrowhead Stadium in Kansas City. Truly ecumenical, it was indeed a work of the Holy Spirit. Half of the registrants were Roman Catholic, while the other half consisted mostly of Lutherans,

Presbyterians, Episcopalians, denominational Pentecostals, Baptists, Methodists, and Messianic Jews. Great rejoicing filled the stands as the multitude sang in tongues and danced before the Lord.[10]

Although Charismatics were encouraged to remain in their churches, many eventually found this unacceptable. Some felt they were withering spiritually while others encountered varying degrees of rejection within their denominations. Whatever the reason, many Charismatics began leaving their denominational churches. Some joined the classical Pentecostal denominations, and others formed new, independent Charismatic churches and fellowships.

## The Issue of Authority

This shifting of loyalties and the forming of new churches and denominations simply highlights the tension that inevitably occurs between the institutional church and charismatic ministry. The question is really one of authority. Must the revival or renewal always subject itself to institutional authority, or is its existence, in fact, legitimized by the presence of the *charismata*? In other words, must the charismatic person or movement yield to institutional authority, or should the institution concede to the *charismata*?

The answer is not a simple yes or no. The charismatic gifts themselves are subject to testing and must function in a context of love and humility. There have been times, however, when the institutional church, through its resistance to reform and renewal, has actually incited a new religious movement. Kung points out, for example, "The decade long, indeed century long, predominately unapostolic behavior of the bishops was a major cause of the Lutheran Reformation."[11]

The same can be said of the eighteenth century Methodist

199

Revival. John Wesley remained officially attached to the Anglican Church throughout his life and never intended to start a new denomination. However, ecclesiastical resistance to the movement he spawned prompted him to by-pass institutional authority and ordain his own ministers based on their charismatic gifts and obvious callings. This, of course, laid the foundation for the forming of a new denomination, an event that occurred shortly after his passing.

The same principle is also true of the Pentecostal Movement which began at the turn of this century. The church-at-large refused to recognize the legitimacy of the gifts of the Spirit manifest among early Pentecostals who had no intention of starting new denominations. The rejection of the Pentcostal believers by the traditional denominations, however, necessitated the formation of new relationships and eventually led to the formation of Pentecostal denominations. Today, these rank second in size superseded only by the Roman Catholic Church.

The same scenario is true of every renewal movement from the Montanists to those of the present time. The same is also true of the independent Charismatics which have become the fastest growing religious group in North America. No fewer than 3000 of these independent Charismatic denominations have already been formed worldwide, and their influence and impact is international.

---

### Notes

[1] Edward O'Connor, "Roots of Charismatic Renewal in the Catholic Church," *Aspects of Pentecostal-Charismatic Origins*, ed. Vinson Synan, (Plainfield: Logos, 1975), 183.

[2] O'Connor, "Roots of Charismatic Renewal in the Catholic Church," 183.

[3] O'Connor, "Roots of Charismatic Renewal in the Catholic Church," 185.

[4] Francis A. Sullivan, *Charisms and Charismatic Renewal* (Dublin: Gill and Macmillan, 1982), 4.

[5] Sullivan, *Charisms and Charismatic Renewal*, 10.

[6] Suenens, *A New Pentecost?*, 40.

[7] Synan, *In the Latter Days*, 109

[8] Synan, *In the Latter Days*, 111.

[9] Peter Hocken, *One Lord One Spirit One Body* (Gaithersburg, MD: The Word Among Us, 1987), 87.

[10] Synan, *In the Latter Days*, 128-129.

[11] Hans Kung, "What Is the Essence of Apostolic Succession," *Apostolic Succession: Rethinking a Barrier to Unity,* ed. Hans Kung (New York: Paulist, 1968), 121.

*2000 Years of Charismatic Christianity*

# CHAPTER 29

# The Third Wave

### C. Peter Wagner

THE CHARISMATIC MOVEMENT had its greatest impact in the more liberal Protestant denominations and in Roman Catholicism. In addition to these, however, in 1983, C. Peter Wagner (1930-), Professor of Church Growth at Fuller Theological Seminary School of World Missions, referred to a *third wave* of the Holy Spirit's work that was already stirring in the evangelical churches. The *first wave*, Wagner said, had been the Pentecostal Revival at the turn of the century; the *second wave*, the more recent Charismatic Renewal, which had been particularly influential in the more liberal denominations. This *third wave*, Wagner stated, would have a similar impact on the more conservative evangelicals.[1]

### John Wimber and The Vineyard

Along with Wagner, John Wimber (1934-97) emerged as a recognized spokesperson for the *Third Wave*. Wimber founded the Association of Vineyard Churches beginning with the Vineyard Christian Fellowship of Anaheim (ca. 1977). He traveled widely in a ministry of teaching and healing. His meetings were characterized by unusual manifestations of the Holy Spirit in many ways similar to those of the earlier Pentecostals. Prophecy and speaking in tongues commonly occurred in these meetings, and various other manifestations, such as being *slain in the Spirit*, shaking, and swooning in a state similar to drunkenness also occurred. David White, a psychiatrist and proponent of the Third Wave, describes the phenomenon similar to drunkenness.

> In meetings where the Holy Spirit's power is strongly manifest, some people may seem a little drunk. . . . They may describe a heaviness that is on them. Their speech may be slightly slurred, their movements uncoordinated. They may need support to walk. They show little concern about what anyone will think of their condition and are usually a little dazed. The condition may endure several hours.[2]

## Doctrinal Distinctives

While emphasizing signs, wonders, and spiritual gifts, *Third Wavers* often prefer to remain identified with their own denominations. When asked if he considered himself a Pentecostal or Charismatic, Wagner replied,

> I see myself as neither a charismatic nor a Pentecostal. I belong to Lake Avenue Congregational Church. I'm a Congregationalist. However, our church is more and more open to the same way that the Holy Spirit does work among charismatics. . . . We like to think that we are doing it in a Congregational way; we're not doing it in a charismatic way. But we're getting the same results.[3]

Third Wavers also reject, at least theologically, a subsequent experience of Spirit baptism evidenced by speaking in tongues. They prefer, instead, to see Spirit baptism as part of the conversion-initiation experience. In this approach, every convert has the potential to release any of the spiritual gifts. The genuineness of the experience, however, does not hinge on the manifestation of any particular gift.

Although advocating loyalty to denominations, the Third

Wave is spawning its own independent churches and denominations. These include Wimber's Association of Vineyard
Churches, comprising well over 300 churches throughout
North America, and the recently formed Partners in Harvest
network of churches which has formed out of the revival centered in Toronto at the Toronto Airport Christian Fellowship, formerly a part of Wimber's Association of Vineyard
Churches.

In spite of the obvious differences that exist among Pentecostals, Charismatics, and Third Wavers, David Barrett,
author of the massive *World Christian Encyclopedia*, sees the
Third Wave as part of one great spiritual movement that is
sweeping the earth. He says that the Pentecostal Movement
which began at the turn of the century, the Charismatic Renewal which began around 1960, and the Third Wave are
"one single, cohesive movement into which a vast proliferation of all kinds of individuals and communities have been
drawn." He continues, "Whether termed Pentecostals,
Charismatics or Third Wavers, they share a basic single experience." He adds, Their contribution to Christianity is a new
awareness of Spiritual gifts as a ministry to the life of the
Church.[4]

---

### Notes

[1] See John Wimber, *Power Evangelism* (San Francisco: Harper And Row,
1986), 122-35.

[2] David White, "Revival and the Spirit's Power," *The Kingdom and the
Power*, ed. Gary S. Greig and Kevin N. Springer (Ventura, CA: Regal,
1993), 318.

[3] Wimber, *Power Evangelism*, 134.

[4] *Dictionary of Pentecostal and Charismatic Movements*, 818.

# CHAPTER 30

# A New Wave of Revival?

### Rodney Howard-Browne

IN MARCH, 1993, South African evangelist, Rodney Howard-Browne, arrived at Carpenter's Home Church in Lakeland, Florida for a scheduled one-week meeting. The one-week meeting, however, became a fourteen week revival with Pastor Karl Strader declaring it to be the greatest move of God he had ever seen. "It was like something from the history books."[1] Spiritual phenomena common in past revivals such as falling, weeping, and joyous laughter occurred nightly attracting large crowds. By the fourth week of the revival, so many conversions had occurred that a baptismal service was held with 1500 being baptized. By the end of the sixth week, cumulative attendance had exceeded 100,000 with many pastors and church leaders attending and being profoundly affected. After fourteen weeks, Howard-Browne closed the meetings saying that God had shown him that the revival in Lakeland was not to become a mecca; but that he was to carry the revival throughout America.

Shortly thereafter, in June, 1993, Howard-Browne went to Fort Worth, Texas, where he conducted revival services at Calvary Cathedral International where Bob Nichols is the pastor. For six weeks, thousands attended the meetings including hundreds of pastors from across the nation and around the world. Spiritual manifestations continued to occur, perhaps the most unusual and pronounced of which was

"holy" laughter that would often sweep across the congregation. Large numbers responded to the invitations for salvation, and many pastors testified that their lives and ministries
had been transformed as a result of attending the revival. The
revival continued after Howard-Browne's departure and the
church continues to see 50-100 conversions per week. [2]

In the fall, 1993, Howard-Browne conducted sucessful revival meetings at Rhema Bible Institute and Oral Roberts
University in Tulsa, Oklahoma. During one of the meetings
at ORU, Oral Roberts declared that Howard-Browne's ministry was moving the Church to "another level of the Holy
Spirit."[3] Then in January, 1994, Howard-Browne returned to
Carpenter's Home Church in Lakeland, Florida, for a series
of meetings. One of those attending these meetings was
Randy Clark, pastor of a Vineyard church in St. Louis, Mis-
souri, who was seeking for a new level of spiritual power in
his life. Clark was profoundly impacted in these meetings by
what he saw and by what he experienced including a burning
sensation in his hands.

## The Toronto Blessing

Shortly after attending the Howard-Browne meetings in
Lakeland, Florida, Clark went to Toronto, Ontario, to minister at the Airport Vineyard pastored by John and Carol Arnott. It was here that the revival, which became known as the
*Toronto Blessing*, erupted on Thursday evening, January 20,
1994. Characterized by holy laughter, falling, shaking, divine
healings, and other unusual spiritual phenomena, this revival
soon captured the attention of both the Christian and secular
media. During the first year of the revival, cumulative attendance exceeded 200,000 with people attending from almost
every nation.[4] A secular magazine, *Toronto Life*, billed the

revival as Toronto's top tourist attraction of 1994.

The impact of the revival soon led to comparisons of the Toronto Blessing with earlier revivals such as the Topeka revival (1901) and the Azusa Street revival (1906 to 1909).[5] Church historian, Richard Riss, stated that what was happening in Toronto was "at the very least on a par with what happened at Azusa Street in 1906."[6] Sten Sorensen, pastor of Oslo Baptist Church in Norway, agreed and referred to Toronto as "a new Azusa Street."[7]

Although critics have disparaged the revival because of the unusual character and intensity of the manifestations,[8] support has not been lacking and has often come from unexpected sources. After several Pentecostal leaders expressed misgivings about the revival at the Seventeenth Annual World Pentecostal Conference in September, 1995, Andrew Evans, General Superintendent of the Assemblies of God in Australia, voiced support for the revival. He warned the delegates not to resist a move of God just because it did not originate with them.[9] Clark Pinnock, Professor of Theology at McMaster University in Hamilton, Ontario, and one of today's most influential evangelical thinkers, affirmed the revival as a "divine visitation." He said, "I go to the meetings in order to wait on God and listen."[10] The revival has found particular favor in Great Britain where it has impacted over 7000 churches of many different denominations.[11]

## More Recent Developments

*Charisma* magazine (Feb., 1996) reported that John Wimber and the governing board of the Association of Vineyard Churches had ousted the Toronto Airport Vineyard from its organization. Although the members of the board centered their public comments on what they called the "exotic practices" in the revival services—particularly the animalistic sounds that had occurred on occasion—this was not the only issue. They also objected to the Airport church's use of "catchers" during the prayer time, the use of lines on the floor to mark the place for those to stand indicating their desire for prayer, and the calling of individuals to the front for testimonies concerning God's blessing in their life.[12] In response to the criticism of the board concerning the animalistic sounds, John Arnott, senior pastor of the Airport Fellowship, said that this sort of manifestation happens rarely, perhaps to one person in 10,000. He insisted that neither he nor his staff had encouraged such manifestations.[13]

It seems that the separation is characteristic of the conflict that inevitably occurs as the experiences and practices of a revival movement spill over the traditional parameters of the institution within which it began. And in spite of the separation from the Vineyard, the revival in Toronto has continued. By the fall, 1997, attendance had reached the 2 million mark with pastors comprising 45,000 of this number. Even though the leaders of this revival consider evangelism to be their second priority—after the renewal of the Church and individual believers—over 25,000 conversions have occurred of which 8-10,000 are first time decisions.

## The Pensacola Revival

Another revival with national and international implications more recently erupted in Pensacola, Florida, at the Brownsville Assembly of God. On Father's Day, June 18, 1995, evangelist Steve Hill preached and then gave an invitation for those wanting prayer for salvation or for any other need. As Hill, who had visited revival centers in Argentina, England, and Toronto, began praying for the approximately

210

one thousand who responded to his invitation, unusual spiritual manifestations began to occur. Many fell to the floor. Among these was Pastor John Kilpatrick who lay on the floor for 3½ hours. He later testified that, while in that state, he felt all the stress drain out of his body. "I couldn't move but I felt wonderful," he said.[14]

Indeed, unusual spiritual phenomena such as falling, trembling, shaking, laughing, and weeping have been common in this revival from that day forward. Kilpatrick, who confesses to having been somewhat critical of such phenomena, says that the Holy Spirit said to him, "John, if you really want revival, don't tell Me how to do it or when to do it. You'll have to step out of the way."[15]

These manifestations, as has been the case in other revivals, have attracted much attention resulting in a phenomenal influx of visitors to Pensacola from all over the world. Since its beginning in June, 1995, it is estimated that two million people have visited the revival with over 100,000 making decisions for Christ. The revival, having caught the attention of the secular news media, has been covered by various local and national news outlets including the New York Times, the Washington Post, PBS, and CNN.

One obvious characteristic of the Pensacola Revival is its intense evangelistic emphasis. The meetings, led by an evangelist and a pastor, are obviously geared toward getting those who are unsaved or "backslidden" to the front during the altar service. One of the leaders at Brownsville has said,

> I am amazed at the extent that Steve goes to in order to get the lost to respond. . . . If a lost person is in one of these services, he or she will have so many opportunities to get right with God because Steve is like a pack hound on the scent of a big buck deer. As long as Steve

senses conviction in the air, he stays with the altar call until God releases him.[16]

## The Revival Spreads

As the revival has spread, centers of revival too numerous to mention have been springing up throughout America, Canada, and the world. For example, Tsugumichi Ohkawa, president of Calvary Bible Seminary in Yamato, Japan, says the revival has spread throughout his country and, in the process, has promoted unity among Pentecostals and evangelicals. In Great Britain, Holy Trinity Brompton, an Anglican church in London, has become a center of revival as has the Pioneer network of churches and ministries led by Gerald Coates. In India, Dr. Joseph Skinner, a leader of the Pentecostal movement in that nation, reports that a revival has erupted in his home area of Shillong, Meghalaya, in NE India. This revival is characterized by unusual manifestations—especially for the reserved Indian culture and personality—including falling, weeping, trembling, and hilarious laughter.[17]

The diversity of the revival has enabled it to cross, not only geo-political boundaries, but also denominational boundaries. Daina Doucet, a free-lance writer who has followed the revival closely from the beginning, says,

> One of the distinctives of this renewal is its cross-denominational character. Baptists, Catholics, Anglicans, Charismatics, Pentecostals and believers from virtually every Christian denomination have experienced the same refreshing—often while standing side by side.

## The Problem of Manifestations

By far, the greatest criticism of the revival has centered around the unusual manifestations that occur. Although many, including pastors and church leaders, testify to having their lives and ministries transformed through intense, spiritual encounters in these meetings, detractors insist that the manifestations are demonic in origin.[18] Others, though not willing to call them demonic, have expressed concern that they represent excessive, subjective expressions of human nature, i.e., the flesh, and that unchecked "fleshly zeal" may lead to fanaticism.[19]

There is no question that excesses have occurred in the revival—as is the case in every revival—and the New Testament admonition to test and prove spiritual manifestations is in order.[20] Roman Catholic theologian, Hans Kung, points out, however, that outbreaks of spiritual excess or *enthusiasm* are a sign of a crisis in the Church. He maintains that the demands of the *enthusiasts* which are truly rooted in the Gospel should be taken up and put into practice.[21] Gordon Fee, Professor of New Testament at Regent College in Vancouver, British Columbia, agrees saying that the fault for enthusiastic extremes often lies with the Church that no longer expects life in the Spirit in a dynamic way.[22]

Valuable insight and instruction for those on both sides of the issue may also be received from that astute scholar and purveyor of revival in the eighteenth century, John Wesley. In the Methodist revival which he spearheaded, it seems that Wesley encountered every sort of manifestation that has occurred in the current revival and recorded them in his *Journal*. Twenty years after his divine encounter at Aldersgate which marked the beginning of the Methodist revival, Wesley wrote,

> The danger *was* [in the beginning] to regard extraordinary circumstances too much, such as outcries, convulsions, visions, trances; as if these were essential to the inward work so that it could not go on without them.

Perhaps the danger *is* to regard them too little, to condemn them altogether; to imagine they had nothing of God in them and were a hindrance to His work.[23]

In other words, a shift occurred within the first twenty years of the Methodist revival from an over-emphasis on manifestations to a disregard for such manifestations. In Wesley's thinking, one extreme posed as great a danger to the Church as the other, and both, he believed, should be guarded against.

Wesley goes on to say that in the beginning of the revival, the manifestations were wholly from God but that over time "nature mixed with grace" with some enthusiasts mimicking the genuine manifestations. He also stated, "Satan likewise mimicked this work of God, in order to discredit the whole work." Yet, says Wesley, "even this should not make us either deny or undervalue the real work of the Spirit. The shadow is no disparagement of the substance, nor the counterfeit of the real diamond." [24] Wesley then says that it may be expected that Satan will also make these visions and manifestations an occasion of pride for those who experience them. He then asks, "But what can be inferred from hence?"

> Nothing, but that we should guard against it [pride]; that we should diligently exhort all to be little in their own eyes, knowing that nothing avails with God but humble love. But still, to slight or censure visions [manifestations] in general, would be both irrational and unchristian.[25]

---

### Notes

[1] Julia Duin, "Praise the Lord and Pass the New Wine," *Charisma* 20, no. 1 (Aug. 1994): 24-4.

[2] Faithe Shinn, Interview with author, Sept. 9, 1997. For information on the continuance of this revival see Dale Gentry, *Revival in the Morning* (Fort Worth: Dale Gentry Ministries, 1996).

[3] Julia Duin, "Praise the Lord and Pass the New Wine," *Charisma* 20, no. 1 (Aug. 1994): 24. This author was present in the meeting and heard this statement by Oral Roberts.

[4] Daina Doucet, "What Is God Doing in Toronto?" *Charisma* 20, no. 7 (Feb. 1995): 21.

[5] Doucet, "What Is God Doing in Toronto?" 20.

[6] Doucet, "What Is God Doing in Toronto?" 21.

[7] Doucet, "What Is God Doing in Toronto?" 21.

[8] See James A Beverly, "Toronto's Mixed Blessing," *Christianity Today* (Sept. 11, 1995); and Doucet, "What is God Doing in Toronto?"

[9] J. Lee Grady, "Classical Pentecostals Wary of the 'Toronto Blessing,'" *Charisma* 21, no. 4 (Nov. 1995): 42.

[10] Beverly, "Toronto's Mixed Blessing," 24.

[11] Gerald Coates, Letter to author, September 18, 1996; Fred Wright, Telephone interview with author, Aug. 26, 1997.

[12] Fred Wright, Interview with author, Aug. 26, 1997.

[13] For a defense of this type manifestation at the Toronto Airport Church see John Arnott, *The Father's Blessing* (Orlando: Creation House, 1995), 168-83 who says this sort of manifestation, assuming it is from God, may be "the prophetic word--acted out."

[14] Bill Sherman "Pensacola Revival Reaches Tulsa," *The Tulsa World,* May 17, 1997.

[15] John Kilpatrick, *Feast of Fire* (Pensacola: John Kilpatrick, 1995), 77.

[16] Dr. Carl Sighter, "Revival Results," Internet, Webmaster@brownsville-revival.org

[17] Dr. Joseph Skinner, Interview with author, July 15, 1997.

[18] Outright opposition has come most notably from Hank Hanegraaff who obviously possesses a pronounced bias against personal, spiritual experiences and John MacArthur who could probably be described as a cessationist. The most common criticism of those who do not have a theological bias against the revival seems to center around the legitimate concern that the revival represents, or may lead to, unbridled enthusiasm with its proponents "adrift on a sea of subjectivity." For an overview of the opposition see James A Beverly, "Toronto's Mixed Blessing," and Doucet, "What is God Doing in Toronto?" For a critiqe of Hanegraaff's book entitled *Counterfeit Revival*

see James A. Beverly, *Revival Wars* (Toronto: Evangelical Research Ministries, 1997).

[19] Doucet, "What is God Doing in Toronto?" 24-25; "In the Name of God," *ABC* Special Hosted by Peter Jennings, April 7, 1995.

[20] See 1Cor. 14:29, 1Thess. 5:19-21, and 1 Jn. 4:1.

[21] Hans Kung, *The Church* (Garden City: Doubleday, 1968), 260-61.

[22] Gordon Fee, *Gospel and Spirit: Issues in New Testament Hermeneutics* (Peabody: Hendrickson, 1991), 98.

[23] Wesley, vol. 2 of *Works*, 519.

[24] Wesley, vol. 2 of *Works*, 519.

[25] Wesley, vol. 2 of *Works*, 519-20.

## CHAPTER 31

# Contending For The Faith

THE WAVES OF REVIVAL AND RENEWAL in the twentieth century are resulting in an unprecedented proliferation of charismatic gifts throughout the Church. The movement now claims over 500 million adherents worldwide and is growing at the rate of over 25 million per year. It is found among 8000 different ethnic groups speaking 7000 different languages. Its universal impact is borne out by the fact that 66 percent of all Christians in developing nations identify themselves as Pentecostal/Charismatic.[1]

The Movement's astounding momentum is mandating that denominations, regardless of ancestry, reevaluate attitudes toward spiritual gifts. Among Protestants, all but a few die-hard fundamentalists have given up the notion that charismatic gifts ceased at some point in history, and now admit that spiritual gifts may be expressed in any age or period of time.[2] In a similar vein, the Roman Catholic Church has given up its stance that these gifts are only for a select, *saintly* few, and now declare that they may be found "among the faithful of every rank."[3]

### On the Fringe?

In spite of these advancements, many in the traditional churches continue to insist that Pentecostals and Charismatics are, at best, on the fringes of orthodox Christianity. However, Henry Van Dusen in his landmark, 1958 article in *Life*

magazine entilted "The Third Force," castigates the traditional churches for referring to these groups as *fringe sects.*
"On the fringe of what?," he asks. "Perhaps on the fringe of
traditional churches, but not necessarily on the fringe of
Christendom." Van Dusen, then president of Union Theological Seminary, goes on to suggest that Peter, Paul, and
Barnabas would probably feel more at home at a Pentecostal
revival than in the formalized worship of other churches,
Catholic or Protestant.[4]

## Preservers of Truth

It is often maintained by those in the traditional churches
that it is their institutions which have preserved Christian
truth through the centuries. Is it possible, however, that the
historic resistance to spiritual renewal by many of these
churches has often resulted in the development of a distorted
form of Christianity within their ranks?[5] Contrary to their
perspective, is it possible that a purer form of Christian truth
has often been preserved by many of the revival and renewal
movements of church history, which, in their respective eras,
have been open to the renewing work of the Holy Spirit in
their midst?

If this is true, then, the millions of Pentecostals and
Charismatics around the world can claim a rich historical
heritage in addition to a sound biblical foundation. Their historical counterparts include the revival movements of church
history which consistently preserved elements of divine truth
that were often rejected or neglected by the institutional
church. Courageous men and women in every generation
have kept alive the truth of a vital, living, biblical faith empowered by the Holy Spirit. That the twentieth century Pen-
tecostal/Charismatic Movement is mainstream Christianity is

confirmed, not only by the New Testament, but also by 2000 years of charismatic Christianity.

### Notes

[1] *Dictionary of Pentecostal and Charismatic Movements*, 810-11.

[2] See Greig, Gary S. and Kevin Springer, *The Kingdom and the Power* (Ventura, CA: Regal, 1993) for a positive evangelical, Protestant view of the *charismata*.

[3] Suenens, *A New Pentecost?*, 40.

[4] Van Dusen, *Life*, 122.

[5] See Walter Bodine, "Power Ministry in the Epistles," *The Kingdom and the Power*, ed. Gary S. Greig and Kevin N. Springer (Ventura, CA: Regal, 1993), 204 where this former professor at Dallas Theological Seminary suggests that something is deeply wrong with a system of theology that consistently denies the renewing work of the Holy Spirit in the church.

# SELECTED BIBLIOGRAPHY

Anderson, Robert M. *Vision of the Disinherited*. New York: Oxford, 1979.

Arnott, John. *The Father's Blessing*. Orlando: Creation House, 1995.

Bartleman, Frank. *Azusa Street*. Vinson Synan, Ed. Plainfield: Logos, 1980.

Bede. *Bede's Ecclesiastical History of the English Nation*. London: J.M. Dent & Sons, 1963.

Blumhofer, Edith. *Pentecost in My Soul*. Springfield: Gospel Publ., 1989.

Brown, Marie E. "I Remember." *Pentecostal Evangel*, 15 March 1964: 20.

Brumback, Carl. *Suddenly . . . From Heaven*. Springfield: Gospel Publ., 1962.

Bruner, Frederick Dale. *A Theology of the Holy Spirit*. Grand Rapids: Eerdmans, 1970.

Burgess, Stanley M. and Gary B. McGee. *Dictionary of Pentecostal and Charismatic Movements*. Grand Rapids: Zondervan, 1988.

Cadbury, Henry J., Ed. *George Fox's Book of Miracles*. London: Cambridge Press, 1948.

Chappell, Paul G. "The Divine Healing Movement in America." Ph.D. Diss., Drew Univ., 1983.

Cox, Harvey. *Fire From Heaven: The Rise of Pentecostal Spirituality and the Reshaping of Religion in the Twenty-first Century*. New York: Addison-Wesley, 1995.

Cutten, George B. *Speaking With Tongues: Historically and Psychologically Considered*. New Haven: Yale, 1927.

Davies, William R. *Spirit Baptism and Spiritual Gifts in Early Methodism*. Jacksonville: Cross Fire Ministries, 1974.

Davis, Kenneth R. "Anabaptism As A Charismatic Movement." *Mennonite Quarterly Review* 53, no. 3 (1979): 219-34.

De Voragine, Jacobus. *The Golden Legend*. 2 vols. New York: Longmans, Green and Co., 1941.

Dunn, James D.G. *Jesus and the Spirit*. Philadelphia: Westminister, 1975.

Edwards, Jonathan *Jonathan Edwards On Revival*. Carlisle, PA: Banner of Truth, 1984.

Eusebius. *The History of the Christian Church*. Trans. G.A. Williamson. New York: Dorset, 1965.

Fee, Gordon. *Gospel and Spirit: Issues in New Testament Hermeneutics*. Peabody: Hendrickson, 1991.

Finney, Charles G. An Autobiography. Old Tappan: Revell, 1908.

Fletcher, John. *The Works of the Rev. John Fletcher*. 2 vols. London: Printed for Thomas Allman, 1834.

Flower, J. Roswell. "Birth of the Pentecostal Movement." *Pentecostal Evangel*, 26 Nov. 1950: 3.

Ford, Marcia. ""Toronto Church Ousted From Vineyard." *Charisma* 21, no. 7 (Feb. 1996): 12-13.

Fremantle, Ann. *A Treasury of Early Christianity.* New York: New American Library, 1953.

Frodsham, Stanley H. *With Signs Following.* Gospel Publishing: Springfield, 1928.

Arnott, John. The Father's Blessing. Orlando: Creation House, 1995.

Gentry, Dale. *Revival in the Morning.* Fort Worth: Dale Gentry Ministries, 1996.

Gardiner, Gordon P. "Out of Zion . . . Into All the World." *Bread of Life*, Oct. 1981 - Oct. 1986.

Gordon, A. J. *The Ministry of Healing.* Harrisburg: Christian Publ., 1961.

_____. *The Ministry of the Holy Spirit.* (New York: Revell, 1895.

Grady, L. Lee. "Classical Pentecostals Wary of the Toronto Blessing." Charisma 21, no. 4 (Nov. 1995): 41-42.

Greenfield, John. *When the Spirit Came.* Minneapolis: Bethany, 1967.

Greig, Gary S. and Kevin N. Springer, Eds. *The Kingdom and the Power.* Ventura, CA: Regal, 1993.

Hamilton, Michael P. *The Charismatic Movement.* Grand Rapids: Eerdmans, 1975.

Harrell, David Jr. *All Things are Possible.* Bloomington: Indiana Univ. Press, 1975.

Hocken, Peter. *One Lord One Spirit One Body.* Gaithersburg, MD: The Word Among Us, 1987.

Hoffman, Bengt. *Luther and the Mystics.* Minneapolis: Augsburg, 1976.

Hollanweger, Walter. *The Pentecostals.* Peabody, MA: Hendrickson, 1988.

Horsch, John. "The Faith of the Swiss Brethren." *Mennonite Quarterly Review* 5, no. 1 (1931): 7-27.

Johnson, Charles A. *The Frontier Campmeeting.* Dallas: S.M.U., 1955.

Jones, Rufus M., Ed. *George Fox; An Autobiography.* Philadelphia: Ferris and Leach, 1919.

Kelsey, Morton T. *Tongue Speaking.* Garden City: Doubleday, 1964.

Kilpatrick, John. *Feast of Fire.* Pensacola: John Kilpatrick, 1995.

Klassen, William and Walter Klassen, Eds. and Trans. *The Writings of Pilgram Marpeck.* Scottdale: Herald, 1978.

Knox, John. "The Ministry in the Primitive Church." *The Ministry in Historical Perspective.* Eds. Richard H. Niebuhr and Daniel D. Williams. New York: Harper and Row, 1956.

Kung, Hans. *The Church.* Notre Dame: Univ. of Notre Dame, 1968.

_____. "What Is the Essence of Apostolic Succession." *Apostolic Succession: Rethinking a Barrier to Unity.* Ed. Hans Kung. New York: Paulist, 1968.

Lacy, John. *The General Delusion of Christians Touching the Ways of God's Revealing Himself to and By the Prophets.* London: R.B. Seely and W. Burnside, 1732.

Lake, John G. *Spiritual Hunger/The God-Men.* Dallas: Christ for the Nations, 1980.

Langton, Edward. *History of the Moravian Church.* London: George Allen & Unwin, 1956.

Lehman, Helmut T. and Jaroslav Pelikan, Eds. *Luther's Works.* 55 Vols. Philadelphia: Muhlenberg, 1958.

Lehner, Francis C. *Saint Dominic: Biographical Documents.* Washington D.C.: Thomist Press, 1964.

Lindsay, Gordon. "The Speaking in Tongues in Church History." *Voice of Healing,* July 1964: 3,15.

Littell, Franklin H. *The Origins of Sectarian Protestantism.* New York: Beacon, 1964.

McDonnell, Kilian. *The Baptism in the Holy Spirit.* Notre Dame: Charismatic Renewal Services, 1972.

McDonnell, Kilian and George Montague. *Christian Initiation and Baptism in the Holy Spirit.* Collegeville, MN: Liturgical, 1991.

McGee, Gary B, Ed. *Initial Evidence.* Peabody: Hendrickson, 1991.

Moody, William R. *The Life of D.L. Moody.* New York: Revell, 1900.

Muston, Alexis. *A Complete History of the Waldenses and Their Colonies.* London: Blackie & Son, 1875.

Neander, Augustus. *General History of the Christian Church.* 4 vols. Boston: Crocker & Brewster, 1853.

Nelson, Douglas G. "A Search for Pentecostal-Charismatic Roots." Ph.D. Diss., Univ. of Birmingham, England, 1981.

Palmer, Phoebe. *Four Years in the Old World.* Boston: Foster & Palmer, 1865.

Parham, Charles. *The Everlasting Gospel.* Baxter Springs, KS: Apostolic Faith, n.d.

___. *A Voice Crying in the Wilderness.* Baxter Springs, KS: Apostolic Faith, n.d.

Parham, Sarah. *The Life of Charles F. Parham.* Baxter Springs, KS: Apostolic Faith Bible College, 1930.

Peachy, Paul and Shem Peachy, trans. "Answer of Some Who Are Called (Ana)Baptists Why They Do Not Attend the Churches." *Mennonite Quarterly Review* 45, no. 1 (1971): 5-32.

Pierson, Arthur T. *Forward Movements of the Last Half Century.* New York: Funk and Wagnalls, 1905.

Qualben, Lars. *A History of the Christian Church.* New York: Thomas Nelson, 1955.

# Bibliography

Roberts, Rev. Alexander and James Donaldson. *The Ante-Nicene Christian Library.* 10 vols. Edinburgh: T & T Clark, 1874.

Schaff, Philip. *History of the Christian Church.* 8 vols. Grand Rapids: Eerdmans, 1910.

Schaff, Philip and Henry Wace, Eds. *Nicene and Post-Nicene Fathers of the Christian Church.* 1st Series. 14 vols. Grand Rapids: Eerdmans, 1979.

Schaff, Philip and Henry Wace, Eds. *Nicene and Post-Nicene Fathers of the Christian Church.* 2nd Series. 14 vols. Grand Rapids: Eerdmans, 1979.

Sohm, Rudolph. *Outlines of Church History.* London: MacMillan, 1913.

Stevens, Abel. *The History of the Religious Movement of the Eighteenth Century Called Methodism.* 3 vols. New York: The Methodist Book Concern, n.d.

Strachan, C. Gordon. *The Pentecostal Theology of Edward Irving.* London: Darton, Longmann & Todd, 1973.

Streeter, Burnett Hillman. *The Primitive Church.* New York: MacMillan, 1929.

Suenens, Leon Joseph Cardinal. *A New Pentecost?* New York: Seabury, 1975.

Sullivan, Francis A. *Charisms and Charismatic Renewal.* Dublin: Gill and Macmillan, 1982.

Synan, Vinson. *The Holiness-Pentecostal Movement in the United States.* Grand Rapids: Eerdmans, 1971.

Synan, Vinson, Ed. *Pentecostal-Charismatic Origins.* Plainfield: Logos, 1975.

Thigpen, Paul. "Ancient Altars, Pentecostal Fire." *Ministries Today,* Nov./Dec. 1992: 43-51.

Thurston, Herbert and Donald Attwater, Eds., *Butler's Lives of the Saints* 4 vols. New York: P.J. Kennedy, 1963.

Torrey, R.A. *What The Bible Teaches.* n.p. Revell, 1898-1933.

Van Dusen, Henry P. "Third Force in Christendom." *Life,* 9 June 1958: 113-124.

Von Campenhausen, Hans. *Ecclesiastical Authority and Spiritual Power in the Churches of the First Three Centuries.* Stanford: Stanford Univ. 1969.

Wenger, J.C., Ed. *The Complete Writings of Menno Simons.* Scottdale: Herald, 1965.

Wesley, John. *The Works of John Wesley.* 14 vols. Grand Rapids: Zondervan, n.d.

Whitfield, George. *George Whitfield's Journals.* London: The Banner of Truth Trust, 1965.

Wimber, John. *Power Evangelism.* San Francisco: Harper and Rowe, 1986.

# ABOUT THE AUTHOR

Dr. Eddie L. Hyatt is a Church historian, Bible teacher, and ordained minister with over 25 years of ministerial experience. He has served as a pastor, teacher, Bible school director, and professor of theology in the U.S., Canada, India, and eastern Europe. He holds a Doctor of Ministry from Regent University as well as a Master of Divinity and a Master of Arts from Oral Roberts University where he also taught in the School of Theology. He is the author of the present volume and his articles on revival have been published in periodicals in both the U.S. and Canada. He is presently a member of the faculties of Christ For the Nations Institute, Dallas, TX, Integrity School of Ministry, and Christian Life School of Theology, Columbus, GA where he teaches courses on Revival; The Spirit, The Bible, and Women; New Testament; and the Holy Spirit.

Eddie and his wife, Susan, reside in Dallas, TX. They are co-founders of Hyatt Int'l Ministries, Inc., a ministry with a global mission of teaching, training, and equipping God's people for end-time revival. Their passion is to present solid biblical and historical teaching that will facilitate a genuine outpouring of the Holy Spirit and release believers into the fullness of their gifts and callings.

You can contact Eddie Hyatt at:
P. O. Box 764463, Dallas, Texas 75376 USA
EddieHyatt@aol.com     Phone: (214) 374-2454     Fax: (214) 374-0252

# REVIVAL RESOURCES

### HYATT PRESS
### P. O. BOX 764463
### DALLAS, TX 75376 USA

❖ Drs. Eddie and Susan Hyatt are available
to teach anointed seminars and courses related to
their books and on other biblical and revival topics. ❖

HYATTPRESS@AOL.COM     PH (214) 374-2454     FAX (214) 374-0252

| TITLE | PRICE | QUANTITY | TOTAL |
|---|---|---|---|
| **2000 Years of Charismatic Christianity**<br>A 21st C. Look at Church History from<br>a Revival Perspective     by Eddie L. Hyatt | $15.99 | | |
| **Course: A History of Revival**<br>Includes *2000 Years of Charismatic Christianity* and<br>a teacher/student MANUAL that interfaces with the<br>book.     by Eddie L. Hyatt | $40.00 | | |
| **In the Spirit We're Equal: The Spirit, The Bible and Women--A Revival Perspective**<br>Outstanding and very readable     by Susan C. Hyatt | $16.99 | | |
| **Course: The Spirit, The Bible, and Women**<br>Includes the book *In the Spirit We're Equal* and a<br>teacher/student MANUAL that interfaces with the<br>book.     by Susan C. Hyatt | $40.00 | | |
| **Where Are My Susannas?**<br>Inspiring and challenging stories of destiny and<br>courage about 3 women of faith.   by Susan C. Hyatt | $5.00 | | |
| SUBTOTAL | | | |
| NO S/H CHARGES WITHIN THE USA | No Charge | No Charge | No Charge |
| TOTAL (US FUNDS PLEASE) | | | |

❖ Please contact Hyatt Press for discounts on bulk orders. ❖
❖ These materials are also available at local bookstores. ❖

| | |
|---|---|
| NAME | |
| ADDRESS | |
| E-MAIL             PHONE | |